Judith Dancoff

The Calamity of Desire

and Other Stories

Finishing Line Press
Georgetown, Kentucky

Copyright © 2024 Judith Dancoff
ISBN 979-8-88838-377-3 First Edition
LCCN 2023920035

All rights reserved under International and Pan-American Copyright Conventions. No part of this book may be reproduced in any manner whatsoever without written permission from the publisher, except in the case of brief quotations embodied in critical articles and reviews.

Publisher: Leah Huete de Maines
Editor: Christen Kincaid
Author photo by Deborah Bluestein
Cover image: *Mistress and Maid* by Johannes Vermeer. Copyright The Frick Collection.
Cover design by Dustin Croul www.dustincroul.com

Order online at www.finishinglinepress.com
Also available on amazon.com

Author inquiries and mail orders:
Finishing Line Press
P.O. Box 1626
Georgetown, Kentucky 40324
USA

Contents

THE BIRTHDAY OF THE INFANTA   1

THE BEAUTIFUL GAZE   7

THE CALAMITY OF DESIRE   27

TERMINUS   40

STILL LIFE WITH CHERRIES   63

ROMAN GLASS   77

WOMEN BATHING - A NOVELLA   89

VERMEER'S LIGHT   139

*For the artist in all of us
and for my father*

The Birthday of the Infanta

I

As a girl, I went an entire day once without eating to walk with the Duke in the Queen's perfect, geometric rose garden, my waist no larger than the clasp of his hands. When we walked in the garden, the Duke kissed me, a brush of his whiskers near my face drawing me into his world of tobacco and male scent. This man who would give me fifteen children and become my comrade for decades, was older than my oldest brother Diego, but I did not mind. He was polite, and I knew marriage to be my duty; besides, I thought in my child's mind, he will die and then I will have my children to play with and a palace to dance in, where I will strew rose petals of every color in the rainbow.

It is alive in me today, this time so long ago in the past. Is it because I am dying? I watch my breath travel in and out of my ancient lungs and know that soon all this will end. The wise men say that when we die, we return to the place of our birth, though the priest told me I will travel to heaven or hell, according to the life I have led. And what of that life, which will be my fate? As a child, I thought nothing of death, only the future that lay before me like some great green meadow, the sun on my young skin, with no thought of what comes after.

You may marry a man or the Lord Jesus, my dears, the Holy Mother told us. She was a good woman, kind in her black robes and paper-white skin. At night when the convent was silent and only lit by the moon, a girl named Maria showed me her playing cards and laid them around us in a circle. She giggled so in the moonlight, yellow curls on her cheeks. My God, how beautiful she was! An angel does not describe her fairness. We each chose a different card, mine snarled with a snake and a shining star, hers with the Lord Jesus. So that was our destiny—I would take the path of the world and the serpent, she of God. We brought our lips together to seal our fortunes and swore to be friends forever. I held her face in my hands and looked deeply into her eyes.

"You are my sister," I said. "I will love you as no other. I swear to this."

We pricked our fingers and tasted each other's blood, though by the time I walked with the Duke in the garden, I had forgotten her. For a girl of my station, the preparation for marriage took months. I prayed often as the nuns instructed me in my duties—to my children, my husband, God. After my walk with the Duke in the Queen's garden, there were more prayers and recitations. I was so famished that day, and was forced to wait until the sun sank below the mountains and my servant unwrapped my engagement dress from my body. How good to be unsealed from that coffin of lace and feel a breeze against my naked skin. I took a sip of chocolate, my first food of the day, one chicken wing, a basket of cherries. My mother said I was too fat and needed always to allow the Duke to encircle my waist with his hands. Other girls were more slender, their breasts small.

Once when we played at the ocean, I saw Maria's breasts silhouetted against the sky, and her beauty left me breathless. I could have been taken for a boy, were it not for my head of brown curls and small lips. Still, in the garden, the Duke said I was a bird, a starling or a humming bird. "I am marrying air," he said. For the hundredth time that day, I wondered if I would be frightened when he came to me, or if, like a sea captain, I would ride the waves of my destiny into very old age, when Maria and I would meet again, never breaking our promise of love.

I saw my future husband one last time before our vows, on the day of the Infanta's birthday, when gifts from all the royal courts of Europe were opened and my brother's painting of the Infanta unveiled. I wore the same dress that day, black lace cinching me tightly at the waist, ruby jewels around my neck, and when the Duke gazed at me, I felt excitement for this new world I would inhabit, led by the serpent and the flesh.

But now, when I remember that day, I think mostly of my brother's painting of the Infanta: the tiny child in her white satin dress, standing out hard and straight from her body, dogs and dwarfs playing at her feet; the King and Queen at the door, anxiously peering inside. Diego's canvas was huge, rising all the way to the ceiling, and he had put all of them in it, including himself. "Why not?" he told me. "They were here each day when I painted the picture—the musicians, the dwarfs, the King and Queen, *Las Meninas,* the ladies-in-waiting. It was a carnival. Why should art end simply because of a picture frame?"

II

"¿Quiere su chocolate ahora, señora?"

A girl stands before me with a pitcher of steaming chocolate and I nod. I have come to the palace one last time, to sit in my place before my brother's painting and ponder its meaning. So much has changed since he painted it. Philip is dead, I am in my eighth decade, and Spain is no longer the center of the universe. Once Philip's empire stretched three billion hectares to every corner of the earth, but no longer. The English have supplanted us, though the fame of my brother's painting only grows. Diego Rodriguez de Silva y Velázquez, knighted to the court of Spain for his service to the King. Painters as far away as Italia and Inglaterra come to view it, to study his greatness and learn from his work.

Diego was ambitious. To qualify him for knighthood, a tribunal of the Inquisition had first to investigate our lineage, to show no Moorish or Jewish taint. The ordeal took seven years—the *auto-da-fé* waiting—that yearly spectacle where heretics are burned alive to cleanse the faith. Today people gather in greater and greater multitudes to witness the pitiable sinners. It is Spain's holiday, to which knights and representatives of neighboring cities are invited, the windows of the houses closest to the burning reserved for the most wealthy. The autos last from seven in the morning till deep into the night. I went only once, where I saw two sodomite lovers burned alive. Those gallant souls could not touch, but they looked into each other's eyes and remembered the time they had shared, knowing that love like that is always worth death. Later the Tribunal flayed a child alive for refusing to bear witness against its parent.

Our family was proven spotless, thank God. Philip was glad. He told my brother that he once saw a Medici cardinal torture a mouse on a tiny rack for stealing cheese, and after that he wanted none of it. He would be the Planet King: his dominion stretched to every corner of the earth, and besides, he was the fourth Philip just as the sun was the fourth heavenly body to encircle the earth. He surrounded himself with artists and dwarfs, filled his castle with dancing bears and giants imported from Russia. Every spring theatricals were held, and my brother was given a private residence in his court. Philip admitted all to celebrate the birth of the Infanta Margarita Teresa, from scrubwomen to lepers, and now she was five.

On the day of her birthday and of the painting's unveiling, all were in attendance: the dwarfs, the lepers, the ladies-in-waiting, even a family of gypsies that lived outside the castle and had been invited to read the Infanta's birthday fortune. The woman predicted only rosy children and gold-tinted clouds for the child. How could she do otherwise?

A servant pulled a cord and a curtain slid to reveal the canvas. Philip stood before it for several seconds, then asked Diego for a small brush dipped in red so that he might make a final flourish, painting his family's coat of arms on the chest of Diego's self-portrait, knighting him in the painting as he would soon do in real life.

Slowly a smile spread on Diego's face, and he laughed. He grabbed Doña Isabel, one of the Meninas, the ladies-in-waiting, bent her backward, and kissed her. It was clear they knew each other well. For the remainder of the afternoon, she sat on his lap as he and Philip drank wine and ate from a celebration table heavy with all manner of food and libation.

Four years later, my brother died of a fever. He accomplished so much in his lifetime: over one hundred canvases of royalty and humanity and this masterpiece of the King's child that stares at me each day daring me to decipher its meaning: why does Diego show us this world inside his canvas that is like the real world and at the same time not? It is a hall of mirrors. He has put himself in the center of it, brush in hand, peering at those who come to view his artwork from behind the back of a huge canvas. The Infanta stares with him, the Dwarf, Las Meninas. A nun and others cluster about.

There is no separation between art and life, Diego once told me. Is that its meaning?

Behind all of them, reflected in the glass that Diego has put at the rear of this invented world, are the Infanta's mother and father, King Philip IV and Queen Isabella of Spain. How Philip loved his daughter. Though the gypsy gave her endless decades, she only lived to twenty-one, the Empress of the Holy Roman Empire, before dying from the birth of her sixth child. Her husband who adored her was beside himself with grief. And I have outlived them all.

III

I will leave this body soon, this shelter that cloaks my soul. At night, I do not sleep. The girl has moved my bed next to the window, so that I can gaze at the moonrise and watch the transit of stars.

A year after my marriage, I saw the young novices walk toward their vows, their pale bodies dressed in white, faces lifted to God. The girls chanted as they walked, looking into their future, toward all I would never know. I was not jealous, for was not my path equal to Maria's, and does not all life lead to God? But now I am not so sure, and I wonder if Maria's life was not the luckier, spent in her devotion. The Duke was a respectful husband and we enjoyed each other. I will speak of it frankly. The seas we rode together were warm. He gave me so many children that on my celebration day, I am surrounded by generations—the smell of leather boots and young boys' tousled hair; the frothy petticoats of girls.

But what is that next to the mystery of the universe? There is a natural philosopher in Italia, I have heard, who has looked at the heavens through a special device that tells him the earth is not the center of all there is, that instead we are no better than any object in the sky whirling in the blackness, and if that is so, only God can explain our meaning. The Tribunal does not burn him, but they have imprisoned him and destroyed his work, and still he will not recant.

Diego told me once that he painted the picture as he did, because his purpose was to capture the truth of the girl in the studio, the dogs, the dwarfs, Las Meninas, rather than concoct a deception.

What we see is sacred, he said, because it is true and where truth is, God is. Truth, he said, is a reflection of the divine.

———————

"The Birthday of the Infanta" is a work of fiction inspired by the painting *Las Meninas* by Diego Velázquez, 1656, oil on canvas. Museo del Prado, Madrid.

The Beautiful Gaze

It takes John Singer Sargent a week to finish his copy of the Velázquez painting *Las Meninas*. He will not sell it; he is painting it to learn from the seventeenth-century Spanish master as so many artists have done before him. He has lived in Paris for the last ten years and it will be the last thing he completes before he leaves.

The room he works in is empty except for the almost-finished copy, and a second work, his portrait of Madame Gautreau, which is off its frame and in a roll against the wall. Next to him is a table with his paints and notebook. Otherwise the studio is empty, everything shipped on ahead to London.

It is late, two in the morning at least, the summer air warm. He opens a window to smell the night jasmine and picks up his palette, but when he turns to work on the Velázquez painting, he sees instead the Gautreau portrait in its roll against the wall and with the portrait, memories of last year's Salon cut into his thoughts: the garish faces, satin bodices and perfumed air, mouths sneered in ridicule. There were thirty-one rooms of art at the Salon—all from the best artists of the city and the world—and it was only when the public got to his room that the crowds gathered. How they jeered at his fully-clothed painting of the socialite Amélie Gautreau, in her low-cut evening gown and the supposed corpse-like hue of her skin. "Below John Singer Sargent's usual standard," the *New York Times* quipped. "A disappointment." Another critic accused him of making a mockery of an otherwise beautiful young woman with his undisciplined brushwork and poor skills, in a painting that lacked all grace. Earlier praise for Sargent had been mistaken.

Within an hour of the opening, there was barely standing room in Salon thirty-one. John left as quickly as he could and escaped to his studio, his heart clenched in his chest. It was not soon enough, though, to escape the look on Amélie Gautreau's face, confused and ashamed, tears welling in her eyes, as her mother hurried her to a waiting cab. "You have ruined my daughter's life," the woman hissed at him, though both the mother and Amélie had seen the finished portrait a few days before and approved it. Amélie called it his masterpiece.

John picks up a bottle of brandy, drinks the last of it, and throws it across the room, but it doesn't shatter as he'd hope and merely rolls into a dark corner. The Salon was a year ago, and he can still hear the shouts of laughter when people first saw the Gautreau painting. At one dreadful moment, a critic lifted a young woman onto a chair so she could stand face-to-face with the portrait. Smiling in glee, she slid her shoulder strap off of her dress and onto her arm, imitating the pose. The room broke into wild hilarity. That is when he left.

He takes a breath and stands at the open window. There are stars out tonight, so many, and he wonders, if he could travel to a distant star, would his mind finally settle and be at peace? He thinks of living on some ruby planet above a turquoise sea. But he does not live there and he is alone. Beyond a few gas lamps and candles, the darkness in his studio is like the darkness in the Spanish painter's vision. He has always loved Velázquez, but tonight his copy only looks hopeless to him. A part of him would like to end his life as an artist and be done with it—like cutting off an infected limb. It would hurt terribly, but once healed, he could begin again, as a businessman, perhaps, or a doctor. He is young, it is still possible.

He forces himself to turn back to the Velázquez and applies a color to the background, but the moment he paints it, he knows it is wrong, mixes another and applies that; turns away in disgust. He has been an artist his entire adult life, and it seems even his abilities have left him. He would barely know where to begin without his vocation, yet the thought is logical. He must be realistic. He will certainly leave Paris. He has lived here the last ten years and the painting will be the last thing he completes before he leaves.

The bakery downstairs has finished their first bake of the night, and the sweet scent of the bread drifts up to him and makes him hungry. He can feel the old headache coming on and he knows he must eat something. He will go down soon and buy a loaf. When he leaves for London, the Velázquez will be shipped, together with the Gautreau portrait. He imagines the two paintings traveling on the train through Normandy, across the Channel, to the cold streets of his new home. And it is right that the Velázquez is the last thing he will work on here, the lesson learned, to never forget the Spanish painter's message, that it is the viewer in whose gaze the work is finished, the opinion of those that surround the art as important as the artist's vision. That was clearly the message. The composition depicts the Spanish painter's self-portrait head-on, peering out in surprise from the back of a huge canvas to greet the viewers of the artwork and welcome them to his studio as King Philip's daughter and her maids and dwarfs stare with him. At the back of the fabricated room is a mirror reflecting the faces of the visitors, the King and Queen of Spain, though tonight John is the one who is interrupting Velázquez, three centuries in the past.

It has always seemed to him to be a painting about composition, about creating atmosphere and ambiguity between subject and viewer, though now the other truth is obvious, that the opinion of the viewer is as much a part of the artwork as the vision of the artist. As he thinks this, he can only say the word stupid, stupid, stupid, over and over in his mind. How could he have forgotten that? He feels the weight of the mistake in the Gautreau portrait rolled up against the wall. He wanted to destroy the painting and almost did the night before, held a knife above it ready to rip the fabric, but his lover Albert caught him. He said it was too good a painting, maybe the best he would ever do. Together, they took it off its frame and rolled it carefully. An American museum would surely take it; John is an American by birth, though he rarely visits.

He sets down his palette and covers it with a thick piece of cloth. When the work is not going well, it is best to stop. There are only a few brushes to clean. His favorite, a small sable, was given to him by his first teacher at his boarding school in England, but it is old and losing its bristles. He dips it carefully into turpentine; takes it out and dries it. He cleans his other brushes quickly, takes a headache powder, and closes the studio. His headache is worse and he needs to take care of it, a dull throb that when left unattended, can put him to bed for days.

Downstairs, though, the street lamps only make it worse. The headache has been with him, on and off, since the Salon when he first saw Amélie's shame, the tears in her eyes and her pleading expression, the moment before she disappeared into a cab. Her shame makes him think of his own first shame, age fifteen, with a boy named Joshua at the English boarding school. A piece of Joshua's body comes to him, his soft thigh and the delicate thread between them, followed by the gash of laughter on an upperclassman's face when he saw the two boys together. For a whole year after, until graduation, there was a glint in the older boy's eyes and the eyes of his friends.

Even if John could have chosen to be like other boys, he wouldn't have. The summer before the incident, he had invited Joshua for a vacation in Florence where John grew up and they'd swum a whole afternoon in the Arno, the boy's body glistening in the sun. That was when John first realized his preference, though the sense of it had been with him since early childhood. It was electric, watching the boy. And when Joshua came out, toweling himself off, John caught his eyes.

They were secluded, protected by a thicket of trees. The two of them sank to the earth and moved like shadow dancers, with no knowledge of what they were doing except for the urgency to put their mouths on each other, and afterward to lie together like babies. John can still remember the fresh, earth smell of the boy, his cheek against Joshua's stomach, and the small golden hairs shining in the dying sunlight.

But at the school, the shame took that away for a time, making it ugly (How could it ever be ugly?) Only the perfection of his art was enough to counter it; being the best was enough. But now it isn't, and if it's not, then what is the point? The night before with Albert, he asked him that, told him his thoughts of giving up art. He sat at his feet, his head leaned back against his lover's knees, and cried. You will not stop, Albert said, and London will be for the best. But John is not convinced. Certainly London, Paris is finished. He has not decided yet about his art. All he wants now is to bury himself in his lover's arms.

The dark night is cool for the end of July, the cobblestones wet.

The baker's boy, fifteen or sixteen, emerges from the back of the shop. They will not open until morning, but they know John and often sell to him at this time. The boy pushes light brown hair out of his sleepy eyes and smiles such a guileless smile, handing John his usual purchase from their first bake. His body is already firm: not tall, but his forearms strong. He does not remind John of the other boy Joshua who was slender like he was, the two of them like brothers. Joshua did not do so well with the shame. He seemed to weaken, and, after a few months, left the school. John hardened himself to it and worked harder. He nods a thank you to the baker's boy, drops ten sous on the counter and leaves, to sit in a small park next door.

He thinks again about giving up his vocation. He cannot imagine his life without art, and at the same time, it comes to him what a gift it would be to be a baker's boy, to not have to pay for the very air he breathed with fame and success; that simply the baking and selling of bread would be enough. John knows he has led a privileged life—his childhood in Florence, his schooling, the years in art academies. He knows nothing of the boy's life, the time each morning he must rise, his schooling or lack of schooling, and the dreams he might have had as a child that he was forced to give up. But still, why must one ascend above the stars to pay for the right to live?

A single carriage passes in the street and a window opens above him. He is a few meters from the park and from its small pond and bridge. Three or four linden trees bend over the water so tenderly. He sits on a cold bench next to the pond and imagines he can hear fish ripple the surface of the dark water. Why can't he stop everything and just live here? Why can't he stop thinking about it? The idea to paint Amélie Gautreau had been his alone, to do something that would truly cement his career. In the previous Salon, his family portrait of the daughters of a friend had won an award. Now he would offer an important study of a mature woman. Édouard Manet had done that twenty years before with *Olympia*—a painting of a nude courtesan staring out from the canvas that made him famous overnight. John is a portrait painter. Amélie would hardly be naked, but he felt in her presence an electricity that promised elevation for them both. When Amélie walked into a room, all eyes turned to her, her body alive regardless of dress. He had only painted decorous women before her, staid portraits of the female body covered in yards of fabric or girls in school clothes. Male bodies were different, wholesome and honest in their nakedness and sensuality: his watercolors of soldiers relaxing by a pond after a swim, for example, their tanned bodies open to the sky. For the first time, in painting her, he would not shy away from that. The thought had startled him, to enter a territory he had not known before. Newly married to a rich banker, she was said to be having an affair with Samuel Pozzi, the gynecologist and surgeon whose portrait he had painted a few years earlier. Pozzi could surely introduce them, and it would not take much to convince her. No American painter had achieved true French fame and he would be the first.

"Hey mister, mister!" a voice yells in French.

John is so deep in thought that he does not know at first where the voice is coming from, then turns and sees the baker's boy, calling and waving his arms as he runs toward him.

"My father, mister," he says as he approaches, his voice out of breath and rasping. "There's something wrong. Please, come!"

It is still deep night. The boy grabs his arm and starts running back to the bakery, forcing John to run with him.

"There was a loud noise, and when I went in the kitchen, he had fallen, the tray of bread all over him. He is just lying there, his eyes open, but he does not speak. I am sorry to disturb you, but I did not know what to do!"

It is hot in the kitchen, the door of the large coal oven open and flames roaring. John shuts the oven door and kneels by the man whose eyes are rolled back in his head, his body covered in perspiration. He loosens the man's collar, puts his own jacket beneath the man's head, and has the boy bring a glass of water.

"Sir, how do you feel?" John holds the water for the man to drink but the baker cannot move. The boy stands nervously a few feet away, rubbing his hands on his apron that is covered with flour. John does not know the baker or the boy well, only enough to nod to in the street or purchase his bread from, on the periphery of their world, but at least his mind is not on the painting.

The baker makes a noise, but no words come out, and now the man's face looks at John in terror.

"Does your family have a doctor?" he asks the boy, but he knows that they don't. Only the rich have doctors, the poor and working class relegated to the crowded hospitals. He would call for his doctor, but the man sees no more than five patients a day. Even if John could reach him, he would not come.

"No. When my mother was ill, we went to the hospital."

The boy has started crying now, large tears that wet the child's shirt. John is aware that the baker's wife died two years ago of a complication from pregnancy. There had been commotion one night, and afterward, the bakery was shut for a week. Another tenant in the building told him. When the bakery opened again, John had gone down for his usual purchase and gave his condolences.

"Then we must take him. Go outside and find a cab. Hurry!"

The boy rushes out as John lets the man's head back down on the floor. He smooths the baker's forehead and loosens his tie; tells him not to worry and that he will be taken care of.

After a time, a driver rushes in, the boy behind him. The three carry the baker to the carriage, and the cabbie rushes the horses to Salpêtrière, the closest hospital, with a large clinic for the poor. In the morning, there will be a farewell breakfast for him at the home of the collector Isabella Gardner that he has anticipated for days. She will have tables heavy with elegant platters of food and drink as she takes his arm and whispers warmly how much she will miss him. The author Henry James will be there. Perhaps Oscar Wilde. Because of the interruption, he will not have a chance for much sleep, but it feels right that he is of some use.

When they arrive, John and the boy carry the father to a gurney in a crowded waiting area and sit on a bench beside him, for a wait that could last hours. The baker is unable to move or speak, with the same terrified expression in his eyes. In thirty or forty years, this could be him, John thinks, and what difference will his career as an artist make then and all the dreams he had? Close to morning by now, the hospital is like something from a Goya painting: dark figures pushed into corners, coughing infants, pregnant women, knife victims. At least the headache powder has helped and the throbbing is gone.

"What do you think will happen?" the boy asks. Even in the darkness, the child's face is white with fear. In front of them on the gurney, the baker's eyes have closed, asleep or something else, John cannot tell.

"I do not know, but the doctor will take good care of him, I am sure."

He has no way of knowing, just as he has no way of knowing what would happen to his life without his vocation, the world that he has lived in the majority of his life. The boy begins to tremble and John puts his arm around him.

"Try to relax. It will be a wait."

The boy lays his head on John's shoulder and seems to go to sleep. John's own eyes close, but noises interrupt him. A fight breaks out at the front of the room and someone yells. After a time, the room quiets, only an occasional moan breaking the silence. His mind drifts back to Amélie because it has nowhere else to go.

After Pozzi spoke to her, she agreed to meet him, and he arrived a few days later in her rooms for a late afternoon tea. He had only seen her at large events or the other end of long dining tables. Close to the socialite, the power of Amélie's body was undeniable, her milk white skin and the shock of her lavender eyes. He could not use the word *beauty*; her profile was too classical for that, but she gave off something stronger, a magnetism that made her the center of every encounter.

Her porcelain cup was balanced on her knee, her face turned to the side, as she listened to his offer, a smile playing on her lips. Her need for recognition was as strong as his. A young French-American from New Orleans, she was not yet fully accepted into society as he was not, and an important portrait by a rising artist could change that.

"Tell me," Mr. Sargent," she said. "Will I need to remove my garments?" The family had moved to Paris soon after the war, and her English was still tinged with the Louisiana plantations of her childhood.

She was wearing a silk dressing gown, and as she spoke, she

shifted her torso slightly, the fabric rustling against her breasts. Society women wore dressing gowns in the afternoon, it was said, to welcome their lovers. Pozzi sat next to her, watching her. She did not look at the doctor, but seemed to luxuriate in his gaze. Her husband, a small gnome of a man twenty years her senior, was still at his bank, but the sky was darkening outside and Pozzi would need to leave. It was no secret at this level of French society that both husbands and wives kept lovers, but nothing must be acknowledged.

John smiled. "I am a portrait painter, so it will not be a nude." Certainly that flesh, though, in whatever he clothed her, would be exposed.

Amélie's mouth turned down slightly, in a teasing frown or something else, he couldn't say. Pozzi cupped her hand in his and brought it to his lips. It was clear they had recently had sex. There was the dressing gown, and her hair had not been combed. The gynecologist was already back in his street clothes.

"I have not decided, yet, on what you will wear."

He wanted something regal, to match her bearing. Pozzi gave a slight nod of approval and she set down her teacup.

"Will I be terribly bored sitting for you, Monsieur Sargent?" She smiled again and seemed to laugh a little.

"Only if you have nothing to think about."

She extricated her hand from Pozzi's and stood. "Then I agree."

As she stood, her dressing gown slid open slightly and he saw her entire body: the long breasts, slim torso, and dark patch of hair. He had seen that enough in the art academies to not be shocked. But what shocked him was that she also was not startled and did not work to hide herself from the artist, only continuing to smile at him. For a moment, Pozzi cupped his hand around the dark patch, kissed her quickly, and then closed the gown himself. She was a woman who wanted to be gazed at, as the viewers of her portrait wanted to gaze at her, so why had it caused such a stir, and why had she gotten so upset?

"How long must we wait? Shouldn't the doctor come?"

Startled, John opens his eyes to the dark room that is like the Goya painting, men and women pushed into corners, children crying.

Of course the doctor should come. If this were his own doctor's hospital, the patient would have been seen by now or more likely, visited in his home. He shakes the thoughts of the woman out of his mind and stands.

"Wait here. I will go and ask."

"No!"

The boy touches his jacket and John turns to him. "It is necessary. Watch your father. You will be all right."

He squares his shoulders and walks across the floor toward a nun at the entrance. It takes time, though, to navigate his way through the Goya painting. All about him are the sick, some on benches, others lying on the floor in rags. He is clearly from another world, in his fine clothing and leather shoes, bright in the darkness. A woman in the morass reaches her hand out to him and calls to him, but he can do nothing and moves on. Goya was a reporter, John thinks, his purpose to force the world to look at the unseeable. There is that in John's work, the need to expose truth, but it is more the truth inside people's hearts. If the Gautreau painting shocked people, it did so because he had painted the power and sensuality of Amélie's exposed flesh for all voyeurs, their salivating stares at the different or licentious, like the older boy at his and Joshua's school. He wanted to push that in their faces.

"Sister?"

He speaks with authority as the boy's protector, but when she looks up from her notebook, he sees only a tired, gentle face.

"Yes?"

He softens his voice. "We have been waiting for over two hours. The gentleman is unconscious and does not move."

"I know. It is terrible, sir. We have so few doctors. What is his name?"

He repeats the baker's name.

She looks on her list. "And where are you sitting?"

He points across the sea of humanity to a smudged image of the baker's boy and the gurney in a far corner. Across the sea, now, the sunlight of morning gleams down, washing out the darkness.

She makes a mark on her list. "We will do what we can. It will still be a wait."

It is the most she can give him, but he feels good that he has accomplished something. As he makes his way back to the boy and the father, he buys two buns from a cart, hands one to the boy and sits back down.

"Here, you should eat. Your father will need you when he wakes."

"I'm not hungry," the boy mumbles, but he tears off a bit of the bun and nibbles at it, his saliva dripping on his shirt with the tears.

"What is your name?"

"Philippe. Do you think a doctor will come?"

"Yes, certainly."

John scans the corridor and sees no one who resembles a doctor. But then, not long after they finish the buns, a grayed man, in a wrinkled medical jacket, approaches. So, he did some good after all. The doctor briefly examines the baker and tries to rouse him, then interviews John for a description of what happened.

The man looks at Philippe: "I'm afraid your father might not wake."

"What?!"

"What does this mean?" John asks.

"From your description, he likely suffered an extreme case of apoplexy, and even if he were to awaken, he would not be the same. In some cases, there is recovery, but not usually."

The word *apoplexy* sends a shock into him for its suddenness and ability to destroy a life in moments. There was a model at Carolus-Duran's academy, hardly more than thirty, who succumbed one morning in the changing room. Coming into class late, John heard the thud when the man's body hit the floor, ran to see a few jerking movements of his leg, and a moment later he was dead. Someone said a blood vessel had burst in his brain.

"But won't he get better?" The boy is crying now, wiping himself on his shirt, still dirty with flour from the night before that mixes with the tears and saliva. John gives him a handkerchief. There are loud echoes in the waiting area now, a woman screaming, a fight.

"We will keep him in the hospital for a few days, but it is unlikely. I will check on him later this morning."

The boy sobs louder and John must hold him up as they follow the gurney, wheeled toward a courtyard and to a room with several beds. The man is laid on a clean bed, with high cathedral ceilings above. It is a place of transition, John realizes, a waiting area for the soul to leave the body. John is not a religious person, but he feels religious here. All around them are equally quiet men lying on their beds—sleeping or something else. The white sheets match the light from above and the white of their faces. He thinks of his Velázquez painting hanging on the easel in his room and his own struggle for so many years to be an artist. All the people depicted in the Velázquez painting have been dead for centuries, which makes John's ambition seem all the more ridiculous. What is any of it compared to this?

He gathers two chairs and sets them by the baker, one for the boy and one for himself.

"I will not leave," he says to the boy.

"What will I do if my father dies?"

"He will not die." John has no proof of this but repeats it. "He will not. Have you no relatives?"

"One aunt in Paris, that is all. Most of them are in the country."

"Then you must take your father there, to recover."

"But they are farmers. What of the bakery? We are bakers!"

"If necessary, you will learn another trade."

As he says this, he understands that he will do the same if he gives up painting. The idea of it is concrete for the first time and possible. He has lived in a tunnel his entire life, with his ambition driving him, and for the first time the tunnel widens to an open horizon. He should like to be a doctor, he thinks, like Pozzi, treating the flesh of his patients rather than simply painting it, but then a moment later, he thinks of the deeper reason for his craft that has nothing to do with proving himself to others—the pleasure of losing one's self in a project, capturing the essence of a person or scene with his paints. He has spent summers in Venice, painting quick watercolors of the canals and the people, merely for the love of it. In a single moment, the reflection of the water on a canal can be everything, and that is the true reason to be an artist, is it not? Not for fame or perfection, but to capture a single gaze?

The boy pulls his chair closer to his father's bed and lays his head on a pillow. John looks up at the ceiling. The sun is higher in the sky. Drowsy, he closes his eyes. His headache is gone, and though he is exhausted, he is satisfied that he has been of some use and has not thought of the painting for hours.

Towards midday, John wakes. He is hungry, so is about to buy more food for the two of them, when the baker opens his eyes and looks at him from his bed.

"Monsieur Sebastian, you are awake! Philippe, you father has awakened!"

The boy opens his eyes and nearly throws his body on his father, surrounding him in an embrace.

The baker raises his arm and strokes the boy's head.

"Are you all right, Monsieur Sebastian?"

Through the hug, the baker finds John's eyes and nods. His voice is soft but he speaks clearly. "Thank you for staying with my boy. We are both all right now."

"I have been glad to. I am happy to stay further, to speak with the doctor…"

"That is not necessary."

Very slowly, the man rises. Though weak on one side, he can move. He is still in his street clothes and with the boy, they begin to gather his possessions.

"But surely I can be of some aid?"

John moves to help, but there is nothing for him to do, and he can feel the void opening back up inside of him.

The baker looks at him and shakes his head.

The boy helps his father walk slowly through the waiting area, John following. The nun talks with the baker and gives him a bottle of medicine. John runs outside to hail a carriage. Hurriedly he devises a plan: he will help them back to the bakery, make sure the baker goes immediately to bed, and find a woman to stay with them for at least a week. Naturally the bakery will have to close for a time. He will be happy to help with any lost income.

The only carriage that stops, though, has room for just the baker and his son, and when John offers a woman to help, the boy repeats that his aunt lives nearby. In moments, the carriage is small in the distance, and John is alone.

Paris at midday is washed out, pastel and faded. Slowly he makes his way to Mrs. Gardner's apartments. Of course the breakfast has ended. Mrs. Gardner is resting in her rooms, the maid says. She cannot be disturbed. Albert also is not to be found. Because the landlady knows him, John gains entrance to his lover's apartment and lies down hoping to sleep, but it is impossible. He stares at the ceiling. When he was a child, he could draw pictures in his mind with the cracks on the ceiling, but now no pictures come to him, and he wonders if they ever will again. He turns his head on the pillow, smelling Albert and wishing he were there.

Albert went to the breakfast, John is sure. If John had been there also, they would have chatted in a friendly manner, just enough to not arouse suspicion, though every person on the veranda would know and have approved of their relationship. It is simply decorum, what is expected of men in their position. He can so easily picture it, his lover's neck in the bloom of morning, and the place he kisses him, the small mole just above his collarbone.

Albert reminds John of the first boy in certain ways—his delicate skin, blue veins visible on his forehead, but otherwise not: his easy laughter and love of adventure and danger is the opposite. Joshua was too vulnerable; John sees that now. It is Albert's readiness for risk and adventure that attracts him.

Not touching Albert would have added desire to the morning. He would have grazed his fingers across Albert's neck with the promise of what they would do later—later, in the candlelight of Albert's rooms, their ferocious, hungry conjugation that is never enough for either of them.

Somehow, he falls asleep. When he wakes it is late evening, and a note is pinned to his jacket: *J—You were sleeping too peacefully. I'll be at Jean's.*

He hurries out to the bar, but in the street, his head is jagged, a hangover from waking too quickly. He sits on a park bench, waiting for the sensation to pass, as a juggler begins his performance accompanied by an accordion. First two balls, then three, four, five, all different colors, spinning in his eyes, synchronized to the too-loud music and now with the hangover, he can feel his headache return.

He is in no mood to see anyone tonight, but stops at Jean's out of politeness. Albert is at a table with friends. He joins the table only long enough to tell Albert that he does not feel well and is going home. If he cannot sleep, he will pack the remainder of things in his studio.

He dawdles, though, wandering the banks of the Seine, and stares into the dark water. It is late and cold but he does not go home. He thinks of the death of the baker that almost happened, and for a glancing moment of his own death and how it would solve his problems. He allows the thought to sit with him for seconds, long enough to know he has thought it.

He returns to his studio, the bakery now dark, and begins to pack his paints and brushes—the sable and others. As he does, his mind floats to the thought again, to the baker in the hospital, and to the other bodies in that room on their white pallets, waiting to be taken, or to rise as the baker did for more life.

In spite of himself, his mind drifts to Amélie as well and the difficulty he had with her. He chose the dress for the painting easily, but the rest of the painting refused to come, neither the pose nor the correct size of canvas. This rarely happened; usually he knew within hours. In the city, engulfed in the social season, the woman constantly interrupted their work with appointments, teas, and meetings with hairdressers and cooks. At her summer estate, the season was over, but now her days were filled with long dinners and languorous teas, where all of his self-discipline and ambition dissolved into sugary desserts and alcohol. When he tried to sketch her, she would grow bored or fall asleep, the book she was reading dropping to the floor. Somehow, he managed several sketches anyway: in profile, holding a final glass of brandy at the dinner table; supine on a couch, half asleep with a book drooping from her lap. For all of her sensuality and magnetism, her lack of discipline was astonishing.

One afternoon, he fell asleep in the heat of the afternoon and woke disgusted with himself. The table was strewn with empty bottles of champagne and half-eaten pastries, tired flies buzzing over the remains. Only he and Amélie sat at the table, the others off for a stroll in the dying afternoon.

He stood firmly, ran his hand through his hair, and tried to gain some mastery of himself. It was nearly August, the summer half over, and he had accomplished nothing. Paintings for the next Salon needed to be submitted soon.

She sighed. "Relax, Monsieur Sargent. Tomorrow will be here soon enough and you can start again."

She did not look at him as she spoke, playing instead with the cake crumbs on her plate. She seemed to laugh, and he thought he was beginning to hate her.

He excused himself, went to his rooms, and began a letter to Albert, begging him to join him in Haarlem in the Netherlands for a brief vacation, to view the work of the seventeenth-century Dutch painter Frans Hals and feel like an artist again. The painter's small studies had much to teach about light and shade, and how to capture the true spirit of one's sitter. Albert was also an artist, the two had met at Carolus-Duran's atelier, and he would enjoy it equally.

A week later, after a full day rich with viewing the artist, he sat with his lover over dinner, and began to return to himself. It was a sigh from the deepest part of him, a coming to rest. The meal was good, nothing like the overly rich plates in the Gautreau household that often gave him headaches. Near his table was a dark green vine, and even the leaves seemed to be smiling tonight, in their color and health. He spoke casually to an older couple at another table and gave the waiter an extra gratuity for his service. The summer evening was so lovely, with Venus high in the sky. Albert said something, John turned toward him, and in a single moment, he saw what had evaded him all summer. Albert was sitting in profile drinking a brandy, laughing at something John had said, and he realized the similarity to Amélie's profile—the long swan neck and Roman nose. He took out his sketchbook and began to quickly draw, down Albert's profile, to his arm, to the bottle of brandy on the table. Later in their rooms, he did several serious studies in charcoal, and when he returned to France, he put Amélie in the same pose. He dressed her in the black gown he had chosen, her head to the side and arm behind her. The canvas would be life-sized, probably larger. The strap on her right shoulder accidentally slipped down one day, and he knew he had found it.

After the first night of the Salon, he went back the next night and repainted the dangling strap in its proper position, but it did little good. The reviews appeared quickly, summarizing the epithets that crisscrossed the air the night of the opening. Critics and the public alike found the lavender hue of her skin particularly atrocious, never mind that the powder was the popular cosmetic for upper-class women that season. "Two years ago," said one critic, "M. Sargent had just returned from Spain. His paintings led one to speak of Goya. No longer." Visitors to the Salon stood in line for hours to catch a glimpse of the monstrosity so they could agree how hideous it was.

That was over a year ago. In the time since, commissions had disappeared as sitters were reluctant to hire him. A rumor spread that it was dangerous to sit for Sargent. "That," as the *New York Times* said, "It is taking your face in your hands."

As for Amélie, her social life was over, and for a woman of her position, to have no social life was death.

John stops thinking about the painting on the ferry across the Channel. The morning is brisk, the air clear, and as he leans over the boat to the churning water below, he promises himself to begin a new life. By the time the boy unloads his luggage on British soil, it occurs to him that he has not thought about the painting for hours. The next day it is with him for just moments, and the day after, not at all.

Part of the cure is the busyness of his new life. Moving into his quarters in the Chelsea district absorbs him. The author Henry James has arranged for him the lease of a studio and apartment near James, the American painter Whistler, and others of like mind. He meets Robert Louis Stevenson, whom he finds fascinating, at a gathering. Oscar Wilde at another.

In the mornings, he sits in cafés by the Thames and enjoys the glint of sunlight off the river and the old weeping willows as far as the eye can see; in the afternoons, he works on drawings or watercolors; nightfall usually promises an interesting gathering or event.

Albert has not followed him, as it is not in his nature, but they will visit when they can, and he enjoys the company of others. Edwin Austin Abbey, an artist and recent acquaintance, takes him boating one day on the Thames. The day is a holiday of sorts. Young women string garlands; housewives promenade under sun umbrellas; boys jostle in a game on the lawn. It is midday and very warm, and the water so inviting, he cannot stop himself. He climbs up on the edge of the boat and dives headfirst into the glistening river, wanting only to immerse himself in that opioid dream. A line comes to him that he heard once from a poet, that if there is magic in the world, it is contained in water, and he feels that, the liquid embrace and green silky vision that greets him beneath the surface: ferns float by, small glittering fish. But he has dived too quickly or the river is too shallow. His forehead strikes something hard, a piece of old wood or boat, and his contentment is replaced by a swelling anger as though the water were his adversary and is every adversary that has haunted him since that damned painting. He pulls himself back on the boat and before anyone can stop him, dives again, angry at the painting but above all at himself. In seconds, he meets the same resistance, this time cutting his forehead open. When he comes out of the water, he is crying.

They give him something for the pain and he sleeps.

Hours later, he wakes at Edwin Abbey's apartment. "I am undone," he says aloud. He does not know what he means, but he repeats it. He lies back down and thinks of his mother and sister from years ago, running on a hill outside of Florence. "Come John, come!" his mother called, running with his sister, both flying kites, but he wouldn't. He was all of nine years old, on a hill behind them, assiduously sketching a grove of trees, a small pencil clasped in his hand, so tightly it nearly cut his skin. The midday sun beat on his head. He would not stop and he fainted.

When his mother saw that, she rushed to him. She and his sister carried him to the shade of a tree, poured him something to drink and smoothed his forehead with a wet cloth. "You are so serious,

John. It is not good for you," his mother said, but she told the story for years after, and he knew she had been proud of him.

Edwin Abbey takes him to convalesce at Broadway, a small artists' colony outside of London. Stevenson is there, James, others. A local doctor says there is a chance, if he hit himself on a rusted nail, that he could become quite ill. John cannot remember a nail though he is sure he does not want to die. Every day, the memory of the dive comes to him, the rush into the cool slippery silk and the loud 'No' in his mind after he hit the object, that made him dive again. He sleeps and reads, eating the good soup of the cook and slowly recovering. He begins sketching trees in his notebook, what he has not done since childhood, following the branches and limbs into the sky and remembering his first love of art.

One day as he is sketching, two children come into the garden at sunset to light Chinese lanterns and hang them in trees. They are the daughters of a fellow artist where he is staying, and as he watches them, a scene from the Thames comes to him, of what he saw just before he dived into the water. As the boat glided past the riverbank, two girls in white dresses appeared holding lanterns, and the view seemed to him so charming and beguiling that he had tried to describe it to Edwin, but really it was beyond words. He did not think he had ever seen anything like it, of so much beauty and innocence—two girls ages ten or eleven, enveloped in flowers and holding the lanterns. To paint that! he had thought to himself that day, simply what he deemed beautiful, but now because of what happened with the Gautreau painting, a part of him questioned if he could, and so to prove the thought wrong—that he could do anything—he had dived into the water. And when he hit his head, dived a second time.

He stands and walks closer to the girls, not enough to disturb them, but to see better the starched white of their dresses against the carnations and lilies that enfold them; the lavender shadows and tall green grass. They lean so intently over their lanterns, lighting them with small flames, their girl-necks paper thin. To capture the light exactly would be the challenge in such a painting. It had been midday on the Thames when he saw the other children, but here it is sunset, and he knows this must be the time, the transformation from day to night, that hovers for only moments before it turns dark. Within that gold will be the two girls, embedded in flowers and shimmering on their own precipice before they become women.

The children realize they are being watched. One whispers to the other, they laugh, and disappear into the trees.

John moves back to his chair and turns the page of his sketchbook, quickly drawing in their bodies and framing the composition before he forgets. He will need their parents' permission for them to model, and it will be necessary to set up his materials in advance each day, to capture the light exactly.

He opens his box of watercolors, swirls his sable brush into a cup of water and begins.

Carnation, Lily, Lily, Rose, the painting Sargent completed at Broadway, the artists' colony outside of London, was purchased by the Tate Gallery the following year and resurrected his career. He kept the portrait of Amélie Gautreau, renamed *Madame X*, in his studio for most of his life. In 1916, he sold it to the Metropolitan Museum of Art in New York. In a letter Sargent wrote to the director of the museum, he said, "I suppose it is the best thing I have ever done."

The Calamity of Desire

I

It was my father's leg in his bathing trunks that first showed me a man's body, the blond hairs rising from his skin, that put a river of light inside my three-year-old body. I touched the hairs and he smiled, and my mother picked me up and kissed me. They guided me to the shore of the Black Sea, each holding a hand, so that its cool water lapped my feet as the light grew.

    He set me on his shoulders and walked me into the water—my little legs stretched wide to embrace his neck, his heart beat against the most private part of me, his strong hands on my legs. Nearing the end of the day, the water was golden. When it was up to my father's waist, he took me off his shoulders and set me in front of him. I held onto his rock-arms as he whispered that he loved me. I had never been alone in water before, but I was not afraid because he was with me—his warm breath, the feel of his arms, and the light in my body—like a revelation.

    That is what love was like for me when I was alive, a revelation, what making love was like. When I was grown and had experienced it, what men and women did, it was as though I was reborn. Many people could not understand why I killed myself, and I caused both my parents great pain, I know, but this is what I must tell you: that after death one realizes such feelings are unique and to be honored. Men have died throughout history on the battlefield, medals laid across their graves, and why shouldn't a woman's death for love be equally esteemed? That so many of us have died for it is proof in itself, is it not, that women are the higher race, able to feel so much more deeply? That is why I am glad I did it, put the pistol to my heart though it was bloody and broke my mother's heart, the bullet piercing both of us. I only felt the pain for a moment. What if only women have the gift for such love? Should that not be honored, valued, remembered for generations?

The feelings in my body were not new, the urges to touch myself in the sleepy afternoons at my parents' country cottage, when they were alone in their rooms and I had grown tired of reading my books or painting pictures.

Then I would put a chair in front of my door so that the maid could not enter, lie on my bed, and reach my hand under my pantaloons, with equal portions of fear and excitement.

Hanns rid me of the fear. He explained that physical love was the most precious of acts, a marriage of our bodies before we would actually marry, and while a small part of me knew that these were only a man's words for what he wanted, I also knew that he longed for our intimacy as much as I did, perhaps more. Hanns was forty, I just twenty-two. His first marriage had ended badly and he was alone.

The first time he took me to his suite at Vienna's Hotel Sacher, he knelt before me and cried into my body, like a sacrament or a prayer. As he lifted my chemise over my head, he kissed my skin and cried.

"Do not be afraid," he whispered. "I will take care of you," but strangely, I wasn't. The memory of the water and my father came to me, and with Hanns I felt absolutely safe.

When we were both naked, he led me to the bed. I knew from what I'd heard that it might be painful, but it wasn't. Merely something new, like swimming in a different ocean, and I could tell from the first that I would soon learn it, the dance—how to move my arms and legs and how to find him there, swimming with me, so that very soon, the light inside me began to grow.

It was during our second sojourn in his rooms that he took me to Steffl, the great department store, newly built on the site where Mozart had composed his Magic Flute, and one could hear that trilling music in the air and staring at their great cathedral ceiling. We had spent hours that morning in his rooms, his scent on me, mine on him, naked on the hotel's silk sheets as he poured champagne on me and drank me. And now on the wide boulevard with its chestnut trees, he said I must look like an angel for our marriage. I wore his mother's small opal ring as our engagement diamond. I knew it was too small, not really an engagement ring, that this too was only talk, but even the smallness of it added to the truth of what we were doing, of our emotion and love that was more important than jewels.

When his business affairs were settled, he promised, I would have a real ring. He had written a novel and an English publisher wanted to set his manuscript in print. After he signed the contract, my parents would hold an engagement party and the proper of Viennese society would attend, to sit at my mother's carved mahogany table, the goose at the center, her Viennese tortes and champagne.

He stopped under one of the chestnut trees and took my face in his hands. "You do love me, don't you?" he asked, his brow worried and furrowed.

"Of course, my Hanns!" I whispered, kissing his ear, "but it will be luncheon soon. We must hurry!"

It was a whirlwind inside the store, salesgirls spreading gowns on the velvet sofas for me to try for him and for him to choose— the crinkly satins and chiffons that turned me into a vision I did not recognize—but the afternoon ended badly. After his choices were made and when I was getting into my street clothes, an older saleswoman with a beak for a nose pulled me aside and hissed that there was nothing really between Hanns and myself, that he and I were not actually married and would never be.

I laughed. Who was she and what business had she in my life or Hanns'? The head sales woman glanced at her and shook her head sharply.

If Hanns saw her, he turned his head quickly and completed the purchase.

It is only now, in the timelessness of death, that I think back on the woman and feel sympathy. What if Hanns, in his desperation, had taken her as well? Plucked her from that sea of young sales girls until she fell in love with him, then left her to move on to another?

No doubt he did, if I remember the pain in her eyes correctly, and the sorrow. As the years wore on, what must that have been like, to wait on the young girls he brought to Steffl and know that his love was theirs and not hers?

Why did she not do as I did? Honor the love that he had dismissed? There is a promise in a man's embrace, and when he betrays it, someone must die.

I am only sorry about my mother, who lay in her room for days, unable to sleep or eat. Everything about her had changed: the age on her face, the color, most of all the organs inside her body, that were old now, though she was barely forty.

When I saw that I was sorry for what I had done, and at the same time, I wished I could have argued with her that the feelings I had for Hanns must be esteemed. And didn't she teach me that in the long hours she spent with her friends when I was a child, their soft whispers about men as I played at their feet?

They drank tea on the portico, the white lilies in bloom, all of them smiling in secrecy as though I could not hear, but I knew, certainly, the truth of what they were saying if not the words. I would climb onto her body amid the laces and silks and sense in their recitations the mysteries that awaited me when I grew up, brought suddenly to life by the entrance of a young cousin, newly arrived from university, or the husband of one of her friends. It was the scent of the strange maleness that awoke all my senses and gave the afternoon its thrill. Immediately, I would climb down from my mother's lap and follow the man to the garden, to play at his game of catching butterflies, and at night, in bed, stare out the window in longing for something I could not name.

My mother's grief continued and I could do nothing. She had found me in my room, my body blasted through and burnt by gun powder, and she could not unsee it, the inside of me, gutted and black. Life had disappointments, she knew, terrible ones, but this broke her. To rouse her from her pain and focus her mind, it was her sister who suggested the painting. It was the fashion then in Vienna, to honor the deceased with a death portrait, and my aunt knew all the great artists of the day, Gustav Klimt among them.

Without enthusiasm, my mother agreed, and when she could dress and ride in a carriage, she visited the man's studio. She was a short woman, but she stood firm in front of the artist, explaining what she wanted, the image of my dead body still in her mind. She gave him a box of photographs: family holidays at the Black Sea, my first dance, school photos with my friends. Her hand glanced across them quickly to keep herself from crying.

Klimt was a barrel of a man who painted naked beneath a long, dress-like smock. I could see that as they met, Klimt touching his organ absently through a hidden opening in the pocket, not in arousal but merely the liberty he gave himself, his body unrestricted, like a baby's.

He stroked the hair on his chest as my mother spoke, in his nostrils the smell of his favorite model. During the day when the models were with him, they would pleasure themselves or each other as he drew them, small rapid sketches that captured their bodies in ecstasy. It was a universe heretofore unknown to me, men and women so unconcerned with the opinions of society. Several gold portraits hung half-finished about the room; a peacock wandered at his feet. Beauty, Klimt told visitors, was hypnotic, as a peacock's tail was to its mate, or a beautiful woman was to him. In an anteroom off his studio were three of the models, naked themselves, steeping tea and lounging in sunlight.

Klimt rubbed his chin, nodded and accepted the commission—a portrait of a girl on her deathbed. He was a professional and did not want to disappoint the sister of one of his best clients. A deposit would be required. It would be ready in a month's time.

And so it came to be, in the long slow afternoons of his work, that I reviewed my life, as the great artist, one of the most famous in Vienna, set each brushstroke across my features and composed my picture. I considered many things that could have caused me to love Hanns so and thus take my life. My older sister did not kill herself when she learned of her husband's infidelities, nor my younger, so why did I alone cleave to the necessity of my childhood dreams? But then I realized that God inside his kingdom refused to surrender his necessity of Eden or make allowances for his children who betrayed him.

It was so strong in me in the beginning; like God, I thought only of what should be and not what came to pass.

When Hanns and I arrived back at my mother's home from our trip to Steffl's, he visited my father to make our engagement legitimate and to give me a proper ring, an antique design encrusted with diamonds that reached to my knuckle. My father was hesitant. It was not a secret that Hanns had been divorced or that his livelihood as a writer was uncertain. My father wanted to be modern, though. He stood silent for several moments, but at last said it was my choice. He kissed me on my forehead and told us he would not stand in our way.

After he left the room, Hanns took my face in his hands and told me we would marry in the fall, when all the leaves of Vienna were golden, and the gold of the leaves matched the wealth in his heart, for what I had given him. When he said that, I felt so much love for this man, and the years of my childhood came to me, dreaming with my dolls of the man of my future, and now he was here.

"Such a ring is not necessary," I breathed as he placed it on my finger, though once there, I was elevated, unaware of walking on the earth for the days that I wore it. Soon he would leave to see the publisher in London and afterward he must travel to Southern Germany to visit relatives. But when he returned, we would have our engagement party, and after, begin preparations for the wedding.

That night, my parents stayed up late with me, questioning me about Hanns, about how much I knew about him and whether I truly loved him. They asked their questions respectfully, but I did not really listen, staring instead at the patterns in their Persian rug and smelling the perfume in my hair that I wore for him.

My father lit a small cigar, its scent of cloves and hazelnut still in my memory. His name was associated with other women, my father said, whose hearts he had broken. My mother's forehead broke into lines of concern.

I shook my head and would not listen. "He loves me, I know this," I answered in my foolishness. If other women loved him, for it was not hard to imagine, and he had chosen me, I had been truly chosen.

The day before Hanns left on his travels, we spent a last afternoon in his rooms at the Hotel Sacher which had become our second home. When we made love, he looked so beautiful to me, that I held his face in my hands and whispered beautiful beautiful beautiful, over and over, for that is how he seemed to me, his face aglow. When we were not making love, my body open to him as never before, I babbled on about our future home and children, all of my childhood dreams, for the first time censoring nothing. And before we parted that night at the train station, I kissed his hands and cried.

For the next several days, I worked on preparing my linens and trousseau and discussing with my mother the intricacies of a household. Slowly my parents acquiesced, imagining in my happiness, Hanns' love for me. Each morning I posted a letter to him at the address he had given me, sharing my heart as never before. He did not return my letters, but I did not worry. Then, two days before his return, his letter arrived.

When the maid brought it to me, I had been dozing on a windowsill in my rooms. So sure, I was, of its message of love, that I held it to my chest for several moments before opening it. I unsealed the envelope leisurely, kissing it, considering it the first of a lifetime of letters from my dear Hanns that I planned to store carefully with heavy ribbons. But the brevity of the thin page carried other news. He could not marry me after all, he wrote, for he realized I was far too *romantisch*! He apologized if this was painful, but realism was to be valued over fairytales. We were not a proper match.

I stared at the word romantic for several moments, unable to comprehend its meaning. How could it be romantic to love my future husband, or relish the thought of creating children with him? Romance is built into every human being, as God is within our hearts, is it not? Now, though, as I think back on this, I must confess something altogether new rises in me, the wish that I had put the bullet through his heart, not mine, and had I to do it over, I believe that would be my choice. What satisfaction to take Medea's stance, to skewer the man who betrayed her!

I saw the opera once, the diva writhing on the floor for killing her children in revenge, but it did not matter: the bullet had found its proper home, inside the soul of her betrayer, for love like that can only be given once.

II

"The painting does not please me," my mother said. "She looks too young, too still, with none of her joy."

She lay next to my father on top of their bedsheets, still clothed, the words exiting her mouth in jealous slivers, the painting on an easel across from her. The iron will in her to do justice to my memory had taken over her being. Her hands were clasped across her chest, the image of my death at the back of her eyes.

"I want to commission another, and this time you must accompany me!"

Before my father could object or say a second painting was an unnecessary expense, she told him she would sell her jewelry if necessary. "What do I care for it now that she is gone?" she exclaimed. She opened the chest by her bed and threw a rope of pearls clattering across the floor.

He was sitting upright in the bed, spectacles on his gray countenance, reviewing the news of the day: the hideous battles on the Western Front; speculation as to whether the young Americans would join the great war; the fate of Austria, which had not entered the battle but suffered in financial depression. He raised his eyebrows at my mother and said nothing. One of my sisters was pregnant with their second grandchild; his legal firm was struggling in the economy and required his attention. When I died, he was enraged at himself for allowing the engagement, and at Hanns whom he wanted to ruin, but there was nothing he could do. My death took a piece of his heart, and when he recovered, it made the remainder of his heart redder, pumping more avidly for the life that remained. I do not begrudge him that, for isn't that what we all desire when we are alive?

He and my mother returned to Klimt's studio the next day with my painting, my father standing a few paces behind.

"This is not my daughter," my mother said, gesturing toward the canvas they had brought. "You did not know her. She was so joyful. That was her gift! Look at these paintings you surround yourself with." She motioned to the canvases on his wall, his towering creations of beautiful women patterned in gold. "This is my daughter!"

Tears ran down her cheeks, as my father held her elbows from behind.

"We will pay for another," he mouthed.

The artist did not speak as my mother railed at him, as he absorbed her grief. He nodded and said he would try.

The next morning when his studio was empty of his models, he sat for an hour staring at a new canvas, drinking what was left of a mug of coffee and tearing at a round of cheese. He was a quiet man, fully committed to his art, who rarely spoke and spent hours each day at his easel, with little time for a private life. Had he not been a painter, he would have been a wrestler, he liked to joke, and indeed he seemed to wrestle with his art, to draw from it the greatest possible beauty. At last he stood. He pinned one of my photographs to the side of the canvas and began sketching in long strokes.

"You killed yourself for love," Klimt grunted as he bent his body to follow the charcoal, a farmer pulling a scythe through his fields. "I understand you better than your mother knows."

I was startled. This man who rarely spoke, spoke to me. Did he know I stood behind him?

The lines of his charcoal began forming into the shape of a young woman, surrounded by a wall of flowers.

"The first woman I loved was my nurse. I was twelve, she forty. It did not matter. But when her husband returned from the Prussian war, she no longer wanted me. You are lucky you died early. Desire is a calamity to us all."

Yes, a calamity.

The next day as he mixed his paints and prepared the gold leaf that he would decorate me with, I watched, inspired by Klimt's quiet dedication, perspiration sprouting on his forehead, and as I did, something new began to form inside of me: a regret that I had never thrown off the pitiful femaleness of my sex and taken possession of what it truly meant to be alive, to devote myself to a calling so that my name might live for generations.

And what would my calling have been had I not killed myself?

There was a time, ages ten, eleven, twelve, when I had played the piano, watched my fingers flow up the ivory keys to produce those heavenly sounds, but I had thrown it off too quickly. My mother offered a cotillion when I turned twelve at the same time as my piano instruction, and I did not refuse. What liqueur it was to don the itchy crinolines and satins, to stand on the dance floor opposite a young nervous boy, drunk with my growing body. The world whirled around me at that first silly dance, but now looking back, I wish instead that I had heard the deeper call.

The artist worked on my painting for weeks, but when I stood back and appraised the finished work, I saw this second one also promised failure. While the flowers he surrounded me with were beautiful, he had painted me as an empty-headed nightclub girl, on my face too much rouge, my dress too gaudy. My mother would certainly object. Why was it that Klimt could not see me as the whole person I had been and only depict cliché?

He knew himself he had failed.

He and his life companion Emilie Flöge sat the night before my parents' visit in his studio, staring at the second painting. They had met when she was eighteen, he twenty-nine, and fallen in love. He told her the first day he met her that he would never marry, he did not believe in marriage, but in an entirely new revolutionary way of life where men and women were equal in both art and life, and she nodded her head avidly. She would lead the revolution with him.

"I wish I had never taken the commission," he finally said. He pulled at a loaf of bread and poured more wine.

"You capture her beauty but none of her fragility, which was the part that was broken," Emilie answered. With his support and encouragement, she had become an important Viennese designer who opened a high-fashion salon and inspired Coco Chanel. She clothed the women in his paintings and herself in daring geometric gowns that were open and loose, and made a woman's body as free as a man's. They had been together for nearly three decades. He fathered fourteen illegitimate children, none with her, but was committed to her for life.

"We let a man into our bodies, to touch the soul at the deepest part of us," she said. "And when you men find us there on that beachhead, you reveal us to ourselves and forever change us. She could not simply swim on to another.

"The girls in your studio—half of them are in love with you in the same way," she said. "I can see it. When I come in the evenings to share your meal and you talk to me seriously, as though my mind and art were equal to yours…"

Here he tried to interrupt her, but she would not stop and she raised her voice in anger.

"…I can see such jealousy in their eyes. The red-haired girl in particular. Ria Munk was not a martyr or a dancing girl. She also had a heart."

III

In the third painting, he discovered it: my beauty, my fragility, and what Hanns murdered.

Klimt worked differently on this painting, opening the windows of his studio and filling his workplace with light. A silence settled around him, he allowed no models to visit him, and I could sense such concentration in his efforts. He had sketched it and painted in half the color, enough to see my face and gown and the background of flowers and designs that I stood within, when he suffered a stroke. Three weeks later he was dead.

When my mother came to see the unfinished painting, she was frightened at first, but Emilie held her hand tightly, and together the two women acknowledged that Klimt had found me.

As they spoke quietly, their heads leaning into each other, I stood behind them, and that last afternoon with Hanns came to me, everything in me open, his body inside of my body, married in spirit if not in fact. And for the first time since my death, I felt sorry for myself for what I had done, for surely this man did not deserve my life. I thought of the rush to find my father's gun, his bullets, to do it before I lost courage. I was so sure that had I been more beautiful, Hanns would not have left me, had I been better or more deserving, and when I put the gun to my chest, I did so to honor the love I felt for him, it is true, but also because I despised myself for not being worthy. I dug the muzzle of the gun into my skin, cold and harsh, glad that the metal hurt, and gladder still for the coming punishment, breathing the word worthless over and over into my heart. But now as I watched my mother cry in Emilie's arms, I only wanted to hold the girl I had been and tell her how sorry I was that I killed her.

After that, I was less interested in the workings of the world, though I was thankful for my painting.
My mother hung it in her lakeside villa in Bad Aussee, in the western lake region, that she had inherited from her mother and her grandmother before her. By now my parents were divorced, rare at the time, but my father had grown tired of her heartbreak and had moved on to take what he could of life.
For years, she came to the villa each summer as we did in my childhood, her children and grandchildren by her side, to be with my painting as though I were still alive, and so did not notice at first when the young Nazi leaders began buying villas just miles from hers. What did she care, sitting on her portico, the blue of the lake sparkling below, that a few miles away were those disgusting boys, planning their military campaigns? She had heard the screams against Jews since childhood, and hadn't she lived a good enough life? She would live quietly in the villa with me and my sister Lola who had not yet left the country, and it would pass. So, she was not prepared one early morning when a troop of soldiers banged on her door, seized my painting, and drove her away in the back of a truck. They took her to the ghetto at Lodz, Poland, where they executed her. My sister Lola died in a concentration camp. My father had died naturally years before, thank God.
My painting sat in a warehouse for years, despised for the

THE CALAMITY OF DESIRE

depravity of Klimt's art, then praised, then at last resurrected by an American lawyer who returned me to my relatives, who sold me at auction for millions of dollars—an elegy to a girl with a broken heart.

"The Calamity of Desire" is a work of fiction, inspired by three paintings by Gustav Klimt:
> *Ria Munk am Totenbett* (*Ria Munk on her Deathbed*, known as *Ria Munk I*) 1912, privately owned.
> *Die Tänzerin* (*The Dancer*, repainted over *Ria Munk II*), 1916-1918, privately owned.
> *Posthumous Portrait of Ria Munk III*, 1917-1918, the Metropolitan Museum of Art, New York City.

Terminus

The girl ran through the undergrowth, leaves as large as fists slapping her in the face, the earth under her feet wet and slippery—she fell, got up, fell again—but none of it mattered, breath so hard in her throat she was rasping. There was something in her mind, a point of absolute convergence, and she would go to it no matter what. She wasn't even fourteen and barely knew where she was running, except away. The Wolves had left her for the afternoon, so fat and lazy. They had names, but she would not speak their names. She thought of them with huge layers of fat under their wolf skin. Greasy, it would spat in the firepan. She pictured it with pleasure. They'd left her with a board of ironing, then cooking after and feeding the animals, like so many times, but this time was different. The window was open, and looking out, she'd seen a bird jumping on a branch, then flying away. Why not me? she thought, just like that. They wouldn't be home for hours. The farm was wide and long and miles to any road, but it didn't matter, she knew that in moments she would only be a speck on the horizon.

Her heart started to beat, blood rushing to her ears, pounding like an Indian drum, so loud she was sure someone must hear. She took nothing, wanted nothing from the Wolves. Left without even a pair of shoes. It was spring so not very cold, but now it was just turning evening, and she wished she had more. She looked up at the new Ohio moon, cold and icy and thought again of the point in her mind where she was running—away, that was its name. She would reach it with complete precision. "I am speed," she thought. "I am a bullet." The train depot was near; leaves still slapping her but she only felt them like wind. She could hear the sound of the train arriving and knew she would come to it if she kept running, then somehow get on and travel home. After that she didn't think.

She emerged from the undergrowth suddenly, a barefoot, thirteen-year-old girl in a tattered dress, torn down one side to reveal fresh whippin's, "straighten-outs" the She-Wolf called them. The pain was always with Annie, but distant, unimportant. She paused just long enough to admire the sleek engine of the train, preening in the early evening light, then flew toward a rear compartment, far from the conductor checking tickets at the front. Besides, she knew that when she turned sideways, she was so small and thin as to almost disappear. She got on, found a seat, and as the train started, closed her eyes in something like a prayer, though she no longer believed in God. A young man settled next to her; she sensed him rather than saw, felt the rustle on the seat, his slight odor, then the gentle vibration of the huge animal starting beneath their feet. She kept her eyes closed and breathed.

Annie breathes now as she thinks of that day, the sheer luck of it, for the young man to have chosen the seat next to her rather than some other seat in the half-full compartment. Later when the conductor came, he bought her a ticket with barely a question. When he got off at the next station, he turned her over to an older woman who turned her over to someone else, until she reached Greenville.

Of course she is safe now, and the sun on her arm feels so good. She does not want to open her eyes, but the man in front of her clears his throat impatiently. Besides, it is Paris, it is a beautiful day, and she is here.

"You have been most lucky in your career, Mademoiselle, yes?"

The pudgy-faced Frenchman nods and she smiles a half-smile in return. He speaks in heavily accented English. She crosses her feet beneath the table and feels her regular self come back to her. French is a language Annie has never liked, but it does not matter. Behind him are the glorious Tuileries Gardens where she will go when this is over. He sips his coffee between gloved fingers, his pinky finger raised in the air. His too-round face sweats uneasily in a patch of sunlight and he swabs it with a monogrammed handkerchief. Black whiskers sprout from his cheeks, making him look exactly like his hound that is curled beneath the table.

She nods but says nothing. Yes, the train was luck. She has told no one of that day, not even her husband Frank.

The Frenchman touches her hand and she allows it for an instant, then pulls it away. She would not be here at nine in the morning except that Cody asked her, always the energetic showman with only his business on his mind. He had winked, shook his long blond hair, and grinned in his way that meant this was required: the Frenchman was a possible investor for his show; nothing else mattered. So, she is here. There is little required of her, anyway, except to let the man appreciate her presence.

A waiter brings pastries, leaves.

"Have you always shot a gun?" the man continues. The word gun is too slippery in his mouth, too personal. She likes this part less.

"Yes."

"Tell me about it." His eyes glint and it seems that he is almost salivating.

She holds her neck stiffly and speaks to the tree behind him. "There is little to tell. We were poor; I hunted for food. That is how I learned."

"Of course..."

All this is true, though of course there is more. The man shakes his head knowledgeably as though her answer has fit his wise assumption. He begins to talk of her skill, saying nothing she has not heard before. Annie only half listens, but allows her body to relax. Now is the dull part and after it ends, she has the morning to herself. She watches a sparrow on a branch behind his ear, pecking its feathers and beyond the branch, what she can see of the gardens where she will go when he leaves. She calls none of it luck, of course, but destiny—that she got away, that she met her husband at the shooting contest in Greenville and then Cody, and has made it here to this extraordinary city with both of them, and is who she is. She was the bullet, racing towards what was always her destiny.

The man is talking about destiny now, in fact. Destin he calls it, explaining to her the numerous meanings of the word—one's aim, goal, conclusion, terminus, already written the moment the child is born. She was pre-ordained to be what she has become.

Wantaya Cecilia, Little Sure Shot Sitting Bull named her, didn't he?

"What was the Indian like?" Here the man squints, the better to see the apparition.

"A great man. Very proud." She says a few more things that they like to hear. For a moment, she sees the old Lakota warrior next to her, the hard foreign skin of his hand and dark eyes. His cheek bones were angled like steel but his voice to her was always gentle. After the Battle of Little Big Horn where he defeated Custer, he was America's number one enemy, but Cody got him out of prison to perform for Queen Victoria's fiftieth gala. He stayed with the show only a season, though. To meet the foreign heads of Europe and show them the greatness of the Indian, this was good, he said, but the white man's way of life made him sick. He longed for home. Now he was on the reservation and God knows what would happen.

"Did you have, how do you say it, fear of him?"

"No." Why should she fear such a person? She did not question what anyone needed to do for their freedom.

The investor puts his plump hand over hers and squeezes it.

"I am married, Monsieur."

"Will I see you perform tonight?"

"Of course."

He talks on about his wineries in the south, his business holdings, what he will do for the show. Finally it ends. When it is over and he has left, she opens her parasol, takes a breath, and lets her hand air out in the breeze. She can do as she likes now: visit the gardens, stroll back to Cody's encampment at the edge of the city, visit a museum, whatever is her pleasure. She would like to see the Tuileries, to walk in such luxury, her toes crunching nicely on the pebbles beneath her feet. Less than two decades before, the castle was burned to the ground by angry rioters, and now the garden is once again itself, women with flounced sleeves and bustles parading down broad avenues of trees, fountains sparkling, young children and dogs playing in the sunlight.

The day Sitting Bull gave her the name, he had looked her in the eye and nodded slowly, holding onto her hand. Cody said the Indians saw some people as given special powers, and Sitting Bull saw her that way.

Maybe she was. As a child when she'd first slipped onto the

train, nearly wild from four years of captivity, the young man who sat beside her treated her with sympathy and concern. What if he had chosen another seat? The compartment had many empty seats. None of her life might have happened. He gave her a jacket to put over her shoulders and shared his food. When the conductor came, the young man paid her ticket in advance for the day's journey back to Greensville.

"I am going home to my mother," she'd said. Little else needed to be spoken that wasn't already spoken on her body. Though she looked ten, she had seen enough to be twenty, and he asked for no further explanation.

Her mother was not in Greensville, though. No one told her that she had moved to a neighboring village. She walked the last ten miles in the night and when the door opened, Susan Mosey, now widowed for a third time, not yet thirty and already old, jutted out her chin for a hello, kissed the top of Annie's head, and went back to her chores. The fifth of too many children, Annie had been sent to a poor farm when she was nine, then taken by the Wolves. No schooling, she barely knew how to write her name. Maybe her mother knew of the Wolves, maybe she didn't. She did not blame the woman, but finally home again, she felt a visitor nonetheless. She was given a pallet to sleep on in the corner of the room and that was it. Two weeks later her mother sent her back to the farm.

On the morning she left, her mother was hanging sheets on the line to dry, the material flapping hard in her face, and Annie came up to her and hugged her. So small, Annie barely came to her mother's chest. "I missed you," she said into her body. Susan Mosey looked down at Annie, her eyes distant and lined in red as though she rarely slept. "I missed you too." She extricated herself from Annie's arms, and went back to hanging the sheets.

That was it. The poor farm was as she remembered it, bleached fields with a farmhouse and barn for a dormitory, but she was not given to another family, only set to scrub floors and at night sleep in the barn with thirty cots and the rafters open to a flock of wild pigeons. She saw it all in a dream, though, because the metal in her back had begun to grow by then, a stiffness next to her regular spine that made her breathe more deeply and see only the future line there for her to follow. Her one possession, a cap and ball rifle from her dead father, became her family. She grabbed it from behind her mother's bureau when no one was looking, took it to the poor farm, and from that day forward, would not let it out of her sight. At night she slept with it, cold against her body, but she liked the cold, her world, the world of metal, that she would now inhabit. She worked Sundays for a month for ammunition, then took it into the woods to hunt game. How good it felt to be there, open to the earth and sky, a halo of blue above. Her father had shown her how to use it once before he died, how exactly to hold the rifle, and she felt that now in the holding, his breath and whiskers next to her ear. Take a breath right before you shoot, he had whispered. She breathed, the air cracked.

So many small animals fell, like they were giving themselves to her. With each death she bent over the small furry creature and wrapped it carefully in paper. When she had enough, she walked into town and sold them at Katzfield's General Store. Food was scarce, Katzfield said. People would eat them. Bring more. Within two years, she had paid off her mother's farm.

Now the woman offered the main bed, but Annie no longer wanted it. The metal, fully grown in her now, had transformed her. She went on the road, to shooting contests and exhibitions, and made her keep that way. Usually she won, but she did not do it to win. It was the thing in her back that called, the line, the absolute arrow of the bullet traveling from the very center of her being to its target.

People thought good aim was in the gun or the hand or the eye. They talked about it incessantly at the contests. Well of course those things were true—the gun had to be just right, the eye and hand like sisters—but really a good shot began between the shoulder blades, right behind the heart; it had nothing to do with what came out of the barrel, so whether the shot was true or not was never in question, the terminus of the bullet pre-ordained. She felt that each time she pulled the trigger—the weight of the gun, the retort, the point inside her body where the shot began and the satisfaction when it met its target.

It is night as Annie walks through the Wild West encampment in Parc Neuilly at the western edge of the city. Every night she makes this walk slowly to her tent, as though she must first make sure that each human and animal is in their place for the night before she too can take her rest. She has not thought so much of the past in years, and it has made her more awake than usual, but the inspection calms her, to feel the safety around her.

She begins by scanning the rows of teepees that house the ninety-seven Indians, most of whom perform daily, though there are also children, women, and old people among them, unwilling to let their loved ones go alone on Buffalo Bill Cody's great adventure, halfway around the world. Why would they, proud emissaries of their culture, to this foreign city with good food to eat and money to earn, instead of on those dreadful places called reservations where the government would have them live?

The row of tents for the cowboy contingent is separate—forty tents in all—including a tent for her and her husband Frank. At the base of the teepees are the corrals. Altogether, they have brought with them one hundred and eighty horses, eight buffalo, five Texas steer, two deer, six donkeys, and three elk. That both animal and man traveled across the Atlantic on a boat still amazes her, most of the humans sick and disoriented, cowering below with the howling creatures, while she could not get enough of wandering the deck in the gray storm, the ocean slick and fierce, battering the masts.

Last year they traveled the same route for Queen Victoria's fiftieth gala; this year they have come for the grand opening of the Eiffel Tower that reaches a thousand feet into the sky, the tallest man-made structure on earth. The Europeans come in droves to see them, shrieking at their performances, as the Indians gallop around the 15,000-seat arena that the French built specially for the show. Famous battles are replicated, except now the Indian invariably loses and the white man wins, to civilize the world. The glint in the Indians' eyes sends shrills into the women's bosoms, true palpitations at the sight of such savagery.

Having walked the length of the teepees, Annie starts toward the arena, aware of the tiredness in her body and growing drowsiness and at the same time she is content. A few campfires are scattered about, but most people are asleep, like the animals near them, mewing in their sleep.

She stands outside the now-empty arena, only the sound of an occasional animal rising into the crisp night air. Today at their show, the roars from the audience were deafening. She was the pretty little girl as she always was, doing her tricks with her tiny waist and petticoats, a gun in each hand. The machine shot out hundreds of transparent glass balls into the air, one after another—pink, blue, yellow, gold. She saw them like bubbles in the sky and shot them all. As if that wasn't enough, she got on a horse and did the same, as she galloped around the huge arena. The audience roared. Someone said that Princess Isabella of Spain was there, along with the Prince of Wales, the American author Henry James, and half the writers, artists, generals, and politicians of the country. At the end of the act, she offered to shoot the ash from a man's cigar. Usually her husband Frank volunteered for this part, but today, before he could speak, some big-wig had stood up in a top hat and tails, and the trumpet player sounded revelry, so it was too late. Cody's face turned ashen: what if she missed? She could read real concern in the big man's eyes, worry over lawsuits and the rest, but she knew she wouldn't. His fear surprised her. She rarely saw it in Cody, already the walking myth, and barely forty. He'd fought in the Indian Wars—ex-bushwacker, plainsman, rider for the Pony Express, carnival hawker. Anything for his precious show. He was a big, fine-looking man, that's what people said—wavy blond hair, long legs, like some tree. When he walked next to her, she could feel the ground vibrate, and now he was afraid.

He brushed up next to her. "Not in my show," he spat through gritted teeth.

She winked at him, smiled, then twirled to the audience, and told the man to take his position one hundred paces away. Too late; it was part of the show.

The audience hushed, and it made Annie want to laugh, sensing everyone's fear that she knew she had none of. The man sucked on his cigar, the arena froze. A few clouds, unaware of the proceedings, drifted overhead. She took in a breath, the gun exploded and the cigar fell to the ground. The man laughed and bowed deeply as his wife rushed to him from the stands. Annie spun on her heels in a little curtsy and gave her child smile—but inside her heart was hammered steel as it always was, and the audience roared again.

Close to midnight now, the Paris night is dark. Time for sleep, her whole body calls for it. She is ready to start back toward the avenue of tents and her own near the far end—Frank will already be in their cot, asleep or pretending to be—when she hears a bleating at her feet, and looks down to see a small kid, outside the arena fence, wobbling near her ankle. It must be newly born, somehow separated from its mother, lost, its fur still damp. What could have happened? Crossing the ocean does not frighten Annie, nor shooting a cigar from a man's mouth, but this baby animal, alone and vulnerable, puts a panic inside her that is hard to contain. For a crazy moment, she thinks of taking it back to their tent, but Frank would not like it, and besides, it would have no milk. She whips her head around but cannot find the mother goat. With no choice, she picks up the little body, so hot and wet, and takes it back to the corral, where she can only set it in the central pen. If its mother does not find it by morning, it will be dead. She should stay with it all night, sit with it in the cold mud and let it suckle her fingers. She is yelling at Cody in her mind that they must have someone to care for the animals at night, when the mother goat appears, an apparition out of darkness, and in a moment is licking its head.

Ten minutes later Annie is inside her own tent. Quietly so as not to wake him, she strips to her leggings and climbs into bed, and Frank's arms open as she'd hoped they would. He is a large man, all warmth and solidity, twelve years her senior. Only with Frank does something open in Annie's chest, and if she cries on his arm, he only kisses the top of her head. They met at a shooting contest—he the out-of-town sharpshooter who offered to outgun any man in the town, but all the local bets were on Annie, and when he saw her gift, he politely bowed and then turned around and courted her until she agreed to marry him and let him be her manager. Not one without the other, he'd winked. Just his smile, sometimes, is enough, his eyes twinkling at her, giving her an "atta Girl"! and kissing her quickly on the cheek when she comes off stage.

Tonight she lays her head on his chest, warm and strong, rising and falling in the moonlight that shines in from the top of the tent, and sighs her sigh, because she knows how lucky she is, that above all her destiny has led to him. Because she cries sometimes when she feels this way and he knows it, he strokes her shoulder to tell her he is there, and slowly she falls asleep with his scent in her mind. He smells of laundry soap and man and the unique smell that is him. In the morning they make love quickly before they get dressed and Annie prepares for the day, putting the steel back inside her. When she cracks the tent open, there is only light.

Today is her day off and Annie will not perform. One day out of seven, Cody has told them; he is fair. Still, she goes about her morning ritual as she always does because she believes in discipline. Without discipline, she knows, the human race probably would not exist. Certainly she would not. She will practice for an hour or two later, but first she and Frank will leave for a tour of the city.

Frank woke early to breakfast and smoke his cigar, so she takes her dress and hangs it on a pole in the center of the tent. It is not really wrinkled, she never wrinkles her clothes, but the same care must be taken each day to prepare herself. There is no iron or board here, there never is at their performance sites, but there are other good methods. An hour before when Frank was still asleep, Annie had slipped out of bed in the cold to restart the fire and put a large kettle of water on to boil, so now an hour later she can set the pot, steaming and hot, in the center of their large tent and place the dress above it. As the steam rises, she holds the sharp blade of a knife behind the material, then slowly presses against the blade with her fingernails to straighten each pleat. She laughs at the number of times she has cut herself at this ritual, but it is unimportant; today she feels nothing except the pleasure of the geometry and the fabric yielding to her fingers. She is done in half the time it usually takes, and after she dresses, she plaits her hair with the same care, then stands before the mirror for a final inspection. She likes what she sees, the person she has created, with all her ribbons and bows. She will turn thirty in a month, but Cody's advertising has yet to go beyond nineteen. She parts the tent and walks outside. Frank looks up at her and grins, with his soft moustache and twinkle in his eye only for her. She can still taste him, their secret, so that if the steel is not enough—it is never not enough, but still—he is there for her. He sits around a morning campfire with Cody and a few others. She recognizes the artist Gauguin, whom she has met before. So many of the artists haunt their encampment, painting the Indians, and even Cody. She is not here this morning, but a few days before the seventy-year-old painter and sculptress Rosa Bonheur, who won a gold medal at the Paris Salon when she was just twenty-four, spent hours sketching Cody and the animals and is composing a great painting of him riding his horse.

Bonheur is an old woman now, stocky in her black dress and boots, but so warm. When she met Annie, she squeezed her hand and told her in her bad English how much she admired all of them. She said that the Wild West Show had reawakened her and reminded her she was still an artist.

She wishes the old painter were here this morning. She would like to ask her what her life as a young painter in this world of men was like, but there is only Gauguin and a few others she does not recognize. Whenever she sees the artist, he is surrounded by people and animals—today several dogs, who wag and bark at his thick leather boots for scraps, and in his hands is one of Cody's guns that he is inspecting, turning it over and over, stroking it, in a way that makes her uncomfortable. At the same time, he is holding forth about something in his poor English; she does not listen. She knows many women like Gauguin, but in her opinion, his face has the look of a broad S, too handsome with a lock of hair over his brow and a thick moustache; he is no one to be trusted. He looks up and grins at her and she turns away, taking Frank's hand. The artist is of no consequence. She and Frank will be true tourists today, visiting all the attractions of the Paris Exposition she has yet to see: the Hall of Machines with Mr. Edison's electrical phonograph; the Fine Arts Pavilion; even a tiny train that will ferry them across the modern city to an avenue of ethnic villages where one can stroll through all of France's colonies without ever boarding a ship. The Javanese dancers in particular have attracted much interest, drawing standing-room-only crowds.

"Are you ready, my dear?" Frank asks, crooking his elbow for her to take.

"Thank you, Monsieur." She curtsies, then loops her arm through his, and together they walk into the morning.

Today Annie is a feather drifting on a breeze, and at the same time she is glad for Frank's body next to her, to feel his heartbeat, as she breathes in the blue sky and clouds and the knowledge that nothing is expected of her beyond this. She looks up and watches a giant flock of birds fly overhead.

To get from Parc Neuilly to the Eiffel Tower, they must take a carriage, first through the undeveloped areas west of Paris and then past messy avenues of poverty, the kind that lie on the outskirts of all cities. Dirty children run through roads of mud; tired women carry baskets of laundry. With Frank next to her, though, she does not allow them into her mind; what does such poverty have to do with her? At last the carriage crosses Pont d'Iena and begins its approach to the Eiffel Tower.

How extraordinary the sight is, the iron edifice rising into the sky. She has seen it from a distance, but never so close. It sends a shiver down Annie's back, the top of its metal glinting in the early sun. Metal into clouds, she thinks; mankind is surely capable of anything. Below the tower is a crowd of thousands, waiting to ascend a very long staircase to the first elevator.

She and Frank are ready to wait with them, but the morning is too warm, and besides, there is no need. Because Annie is who she is, the mayor of Paris has extended an invitation for a night visit, for any evening they choose. They will go in a week, after the American Gala. They turn in the opposite direction and walk through the Champ de Mars, a landscape of gardens and fountains, decorated throughout with Mr. Edison's incandescent bulbs. At night, people say, he has made the city glow. At the end of the garden, they take their seats in the small train that will carry them to the villages the city has created to represent all of the colonies of France, and soon Annie can smell the quarter even before it comes into view.

It is not really a quarter, of course, but an exhibition of small huts and buildings set within the modern city, and guarded over by an impressive colonial mansion, with guards at the ready, their bayonets drawn. The steel of the bayonets glints in the sun, and at the same time, swirling around the metal, are all the fragrances and songs of faraway places she has only dreamt of.

To enter the quarter, one must walk through the arch of the impressive colonial mansion, built especially for the Exposition and guarded over by the bayonets. Beyond the arch, golden minarets come into view, Cambodian temples, Egyptian domes, exhibits from Cairo to the Americas and beyond, and off to one side, an African hut of half-naked women, enclosed in a cage-like fence. The breasts of the women swing openly, infants suckling. In front of the cage, a cluster of dainty French schoolgirls holds out sweet lozenges and bonbons to their naked counterparts on the other side. A small boy takes one, his eyes round, and the girls squeal and run away. Further on, veiled matrons rush across the road to a small mosque while young boys lead donkeys to market, crying out in strange foreign tongues.

To colonize is to own; Annie knows this. It is what stronger countries do to weaker ones, what the white man has done to the Indian, and besides is the way of the world. She has no opinion about this and at the same time all limitations of freedom cause in her a feeling of great discomfort. The day before, the King of Senegal went to Cody to ask if he could buy her as one of his wives.

He was sitting on a bale of hay in one of the small corrals off the arena waiting to go on. She had just finished the cigar act.

"Should have sold you to the King of Senegal," he winked. His eyes were twinkling.

Outside the small corral, the arena was alive with the buffalo stampede—five animals in all—to be followed by the wagon-train-Indian-ambush, saved, in short order, by none other than Buffalo Bill himself.

She grinned to show that she didn't take him seriously and took off her guns. She set them on a table and began washing gun powder from her hands.

"Oh, he offered, all right. There was some little man with him in his entourage who spoke English. One million US dollars to buy you as a wife." Cody's eyes glowed. "I told 'em you were far too much trouble, that you'd probably shoot him or something, but he said they had ways of dealing with such women. 'In that case,' I answered, 'I'll take two million.'"

Annie had laughed, but strapped her guns back on and did not wait for him to go on as she usually did.

Now she and Frank take their seats at the Javanese theater just as the performance is starting. The dancers are the stars of the ethnic village, people say. The musicians cannot get enough, nor the artists and writers. There is a hushed anticipation, and then the curtain separates to reveal a line of seated musicians. The bells are the first to begin, soft crystalline sounds that rise in pitch and tempo followed by a patter of drums, then louder and louder, and in moments Annie is transported to an ocean of sound. "It is called gamelan music," Frank whispers in her ear. He clutches her hand and kisses it. "Look." Near the stage is a European man closely inspecting the instruments and taking notes. "That's the composer, Claude Debussy. They say he comes everyday. That he cannot stay away."

The music ocean reminds Annie of the glass balls they shoot into the air for her—lavender, gold, cyan—fragile shapes that she shoots into a zillion pieces, and behind the first row of instruments are the animal drums, whispering at first, then increasingly loud. She closes her eyes to see the colors and drums move in the black space behind her eyes. When she opens them, a troupe of young girls is dancing on the stage. Each is a shimmer of gold, her hands turned in intricate curlicues, her head tilted beneath a jeweled crown. In her entire life, Annie has never seen anything so beautiful.

When the performance ends, she and Frank along with others who are recognized are invited into the dancers' small dressing-room-tent behind the stage. Everything here is aglow: the candles scattered about, the sheen of a red velvet curtain, above all the girls themselves in their gold cummerbunds and pantaloons, skin of the finest copper. If only Bonheur were here; Annie would feel comfortable talking to her, but she is shy with people she does not know. She seats herself in front of a long mirror and for the moment simply watches the small party through the glass. Frank talks with Debussy and other artists. Gauguin is near the front of the tent with the troupe's overseer, a short Dutchman in a crooked white wig and embroidered leggings. He is smoking a cigarette from a long, pearl holder. His lips are crimson, face powdered nearly blue. He twists one embroidered leg round the other like a girl though he must be close to sixty, and feeds a small canary in a golden cage, then lifts a glass of champagne.

"Mesdames et Messieurs, welcome to our boudoir!"

He repeats himself in French, uncorks another bottle and refills glasses. Gauguin raises his glass, gesturing broadly. The tent is almost too small for him, his head brushing the top. His voice booms out in French and it is clear he is making some effusive compliment. The Dutchman tilts his head down and blushes, then snaps something at an older child, who moves to Gauguin, her eyes on the floor, and touches his hand.

Gauguin laughs, kisses her on the neck, and takes her with him to a stool in the corner. It sickens Annie; she has seen enough. She looks toward Frank. It is time to go. The youngest of the girls, perhaps not more than ten, comes up next to her. The girl dips her fingers into a pearl make-up box that sits before the mirror and pulls out lip rouge.

"Is this your make-up?" Annie asks. The girl does not speak English, but Annie would like to talk to her, be close to her dewy skin and the obsidian of her hair. In spite of herself, Annie glances into the mirror again and sees the painter now nuzzling the older girl's neck. The girl says something, and he throws his head back in a laugh. When he opens his mouth, it is red and huge, the mouth of an animal.

"No Madame," the child whispers.

"Oh, you speak English?"

"A little."

Her voice is so soft, Annie can barely hear. Now the painter is pouring the older girl a glass of champagne and encouraging her to drink. She brings the glass to her mouth, giggling at the fizz of bubbles.

"Are you Annie Oakley?" the child asks. She begins to paint her lips with a tiny finger.

"Yes."

"Will you teach me the gun?"

That makes her feel better, that a child should learn protection. "If you like. What would you like to know?"

"How to shoot the bubbles."

She means the glass balls they shoot into the air. The girl takes a brush and begins to powder her cheeks. Her eyelids are like some kind of flower petal, Annie thinks, the green stuff of life still on them. She can sense the weight and substance of the girl, the veins on the girl's tiny neck pumping softly, a lemon scent rising off her skin. Was she ever that small? When Annie was that age, she was with the Wolves. One winter night the She-Wolf locked her outside. It was so cold and snowed so hard that in the morning, Annie's feet were nearly frozen. After they let her back in, she was sick for a month.

The girl sits on her lap and puts an arm around her shoulder. It is done before Annie can stop her. A small monkey jumps on the girl's lap and she gives it something to eat. Her bare feet, covered in rings and anklets, swing against Annie's skirts. Annie closes her eyes in such pleasure, to feel the girl so close, the small bundle of her body next to her own. She would like to stroke her, run her hand over her body, but the most she can manage is to shadow her body with her hand.

The feeling of the dressing room stays with Annie for hours. It is black night now, not even a moon shining above, and still she cannot sleep. Frank lies beside her, his large chest rising and falling in a steady rhythm, the distant sounds of the animals like a gentle curtain, but none of it does any good.

She thinks of the small goat from the other night and wonders if it lived; a part of her would like to rush to find out, and she must forcibly stop herself. She can smell morning. It has been years since she has not slept. Something to do with the dressing room, though she hardly knows. In her mind are only images: first of the child moving so quickly onto her lap—so precious, how she would have liked to hold onto her forever—and then through the mirror, the counter-image of the dog-man licking at the older girl's neck.

After they returned, she tried to talk to Frank about it, but she could barely find the words. "I don't think the children are well cared for," she started.

"Oh? They seem in good health."

He undressed to his leggings and climbed into bed, smiling at her with his soft eyes and patting at the spot that was Annie's spot. It was the place next to him where she laid her head each night and drifted into sleep, but tonight she knew there would be no drifting.

Through a slit in their tent, she had looked at the careful rows of other tents and teepees that she was so glad of—neat, symmetrical, like the line of a bullet. She did not think she wanted to revisit Paris for days. She pictured the head of the child on her lap, the rows of symmetrical ebony braids, and the shiny white scalp between.

"Annie?"

She said nothing.

"We can take in a child, you know, if you would like. When we get back." This was not the first time they had talked about this. To Annie, though, a child meant responsibility and care; they did not live that kind of life. Luckily, she had never gotten pregnant, they both believed because of the night she was frozen. To Frank a child was unimportant. She was everything to him he said. He only wanted what she wanted.

"That's not it, Frank." She sat on the bed next to him, tears at the rim of her eyes. "Why was Gauguin there? Is it true he has them pose?"

"I have heard that."

"Is there nothing that can be done to stop him?"

"I don't think so."

Frank stroked her face wiping away her tears, but did not speak further.

Now it is morning. She walks outside the tent to the few campfires just starting, the images of the two girls still haunting her and for the first time she is homesick for Ohio, though it will be weeks before they can go home.

It is like the hammer and barrel of Annie's shotgun has come undone; that is how she feels. She can almost hear the metal clicks, the many parts of the shotgun falling to the floor, and there is no one who can put it back together.

She misses two targets at her performance that day because she has not slept, but then it happens several days in a row. She cuts the cigar act from the routine entirely and will not attempt it again while she is in Paris. Red Shirt, the young Lakota medicine man, comes to her after a particularly bad performance. He has seen the problem as others have. Maybe Cody has sent him. He seats her across from him on a bale of hay, holds both her hands and begins to chant. How can this help, she thinks, but she keeps her eyes closed and feels his hand touch her forehead. His body is so cool and smooth; she can feel his coolness and smoothness enter her, his chant moving through her body. He lays her down on the bale, covers her with a blanket, and rubs something on her forehead that makes her sleep.

After that, the week is less dreadful; her performances are not perfect, but they are passable; she sleeps again through the night. When the week is over, she is one week closer to going back to Ohio, and in addition she and Frank will go tonight to the American Gala at the Grand Colonial Palace. The Mayor of Paris will be there, to crown Edison and pay homage to the American contingent, and when it is over, she and Frank will be allowed their night visit to the Eiffel Tower.

She spends the day visiting friends and at target practice, missing nothing. As evening approaches, she dresses in her best buckskin skirts, plaiting her hair carefully and knotting Frank's tie as he loves her to do. That night as she enters the palace on his arm, gliding into a sea of perfume and tuxedos, an orchestra plays the latest tunes, and in spite of herself, she sighs. If fifty meters away half-naked Africans shiver in the night air, it is unknown here. A row of Edison's electrical chandeliers hangs above them like stars, and everywhere are celebrities: the actress Sarah Bernhardt, the writer Oscar Wilde, the Prince of Wales. She and Frank twirl through three waltzes, then stop for champagne as the actress approaches. Annie knows it is Bernhardt by her trademark profile and the way her auburn hair falls on her translucent skin. She wears a diaphanous dress of musk chiffon, a long string of pearls twisting through her fingers.

My God her skin is soft, like some kind of angel, Annie thinks, and a sweet scent rises off her body. She stays just long enough to compliment Annie on her show, eyes twinkling, then floats off to another group, her perfume wafting behind her. She and Frank are about to dance again when the waltz ends and the orchestra begins a special introduction. Thomas Edison—it must be him, Annie realizes, though she has not met him before—moves to the front of the ballroom. He is a neat, middle-aged man with a barrel chest and a gold watch dangling from his vest, a petite, gray-haired wife on his arm. He looks like any businessman, and yet he is not any businessman; he has already remade the world. Next to Edison is the mayor of the city, a shorter businessman in a fancier suit, but otherwise little different. The mayor gives a brief, heavily accented speech about Edison's greatness and about the greatness of America for its inventiveness and genius, then christens Edison the King of Light, and the room breaks into applause.

It is cool outside and quiet. The stars are in their places and the animals of the earth content.

Before they make their night visit to the Eiffel Tower, she and Frank will stop at the Javanese compound since Frank has promised to mail some of the Dutchman's letters via the American post. Annie suggests they also visit the dancers' tent and Frank readily agrees. When she was at the poorhouse, a troop of matrons would march through monthly to check on their clothing and food. The director would have them wash in icy water and stand for inspection. The image of that crosses her mind, but she quickly dismisses it. Soon enough, she and Frank are inside the Javanese compound, and Annie is sitting beside the bed of the youngest child.

It is dark in the tent, the dancers fast asleep, why did she think it would be otherwise? Frank is busy, though, so she will have to wait for him here, watching as the chest of the smallest dancer moves in and out in steady breaths. There is nothing to see here, surely;

she can still feel the contentment of the world outside the tent, as though it is a breath of air from God.

The girl turns in her sleep, and Annie strokes her arm, then smooths the covers under her chin. She never thinks of the children she did not have, but next to the girl, she feels the lack—what it might have been like and what it would have given her.

The girl quiets. Is she happy in her life? Unhappy? Her pearlized cheeks tell her nothing, nor the thick black eyelashes that close her eyelids. Youth is too beautiful, Annie realizes; it hides the reality of what exists beneath.

Fifteen minutes later Annie is outside the compound, still waiting for Frank. She breathes in the brisk scent of jasmine surrounding the camp and behind that the dampness in the air that foretells a late-night shower. It is as though the very molecules in the air are asleep tonight. She looks up at the stars again and thinks how foolish she was to worry. All childhoods are not her childhood. Still, she decides that when they are back home, she will start a charity for orphan girls, to support their education. The idea makes her smile, the small imaginings of what she might call it and all the good she will do, so it takes her a moment to register the new sound in the air, something like the scuffling made by a small animal.

She is sure it is that until the higher pitch comes in, the unmistakable thrumbeat of fear that draws Annie towards a smaller side tent a distance away from the Javanese tent, the sound growing louder with each foot she draws closer.

Somewhere within five feet of the small tent opening, Annie recognizes it as the voice of a human child, and now her own heart joins in, pounding in her ears. She pulls back the flap of the tent and is met by the gaze of a dark-skinned Javanese girl, perhaps eleven or twelve. Not one of the dancers—her features are too native-like and black for that, her face so alive with terror that it looks as though the whites of the girl's eyes are about to roll out. Nothing makes sense, all jumbled and strange. She is half-dressed in some kind of strange costume of a Dutch farm woman, but nearly fallen off her tiny body, and when she sees Annie, the child rushes to her and clutches her hand in such a terrible vise that Annie is caught immobile—unable to see beyond the girl's gaze.

The eyes are the eyes of a child, Annie thinks, but around them swim a red-rimmed sea of woe that she knows all too well.

"No, no!" the Dutchman barks at the child. He startles Annie, coming up behind her from out of the night, his chest against her back for God's sake, and shouting in some foreign tongue at the tiny girl as she digs her vise deeper and deeper into Annie's hand.

The man must have walked Frank to the exit of the Javanese compound, and then, seeing her encounter with the child, rushed over to solve it. But he is solving nothing, so close to Annie now that his entire body melds into her back. She has never been this close to a man other than Frank and it makes her want to vomit, his crumbling ribcage and hot, knotted heart moving against her spine. His breath comes out next to Annie's ear, warm and terrible smelling. The girl has Annie's hands from the front so it is difficult, but Annie twists her neck back to confront the man, his ridiculous powdered face swollen in rage, the wig halfway down his blue cheek.

"What are you doing?" she screams. "Let her go!"

"I apologize Miss Oakley. I will break her hand if need be." Now he reaches more tightly around Annie, a full lover's embrace, to find the girl's hand and work at pulling back individual fingers. It is sickening, his body so close. Even without the girl, it would be sickening. It is hard for Annie to breathe.

"No! Stop!"

With her free hand, she pushes at his chest, to get him away from both of them. Somehow, though, a small finger is bent back too far, and the girl shrieks in pain.

"What is the problem?" Frank is at their sides, trying to enter the struggling triumvirate, but there is no room.

The Dutchman shouts something new to the girl, loud bursts of spatted air, over and over against Annie's ear, his spit on her cheek, and slowly it takes effect. In front of her, Annie can watch as the child's eyes seem to break, the lids drifting down, the vise loosened. Her whole body shifts, in fact, the fire draining out of it. She was a girl and now she is a shadow, backing into the tent.

Annie wants to chase in after her, but the man holds her back. "She came to him herself," he says, "and asked for work. Otherwise she and her brother would be on the streets. She is well paid; do not worry."

The man lets her go. "It is nothing so terrible," he says, entering the tent after the child.

Now that the girl is inside, no one seems to care what Annie sees. The tent is empty except for a small chaise lounge in its center lit with candles and, in front of it, the back of an artist's easel. Annie can see neither the painting nor the man, though she does not need to. It is clear merely by his shoes, wide and implacable, and the smell of his tobacco.

The Dutchman walks the girl to the chaise. He whispers into the child's ear and leads her into position, then pulls the dress from her shoulders to reveal the tiny pin-points of her half-formed breasts.

It is then that the S face looks out from behind his canvas and grins at Annie, winking only once.

Why does she not have her pistol at such times, so that she can carry out the justice that is necessary, then grab the girl's hand and rush with her somewhere away? Annie fixes her gaze on the child's feet since she has not the heart to look elsewhere. She would bathe the feet in scented water and carnations, and afterwards when the girl was tired, put her in a feather bed.

"Come, Annie," Frank whispers behind her, but she refuses to listen. "Come."

He takes her hand, the hand caught in the vise that she can still feel, but the pain is pleasure because it is the shadow of the girl trying to free herself that Annie would like to keep alive forever. To colonize is to own, to hollow out fully until there is only the flag of the other existing inside you.

"Come."

She hears nothing until she is standing on top of the Eiffel Tower with him, the farthest away that any human being can travel on earth. Yes, there are certain mountains, but no one has yet scaled them. That would be a good idea, to take all the children in need to such a mountain so they will not be harmed.

She has no memory of ascending the Tower, but it is colder here, and closer to the stars. They are alone, this night visit the mayor's gift, with a bottle of champagne and Mr. Edison's gramophone to play, but none of that matters now. Paris is aglow below her, the world modern and made new, but she looks at nothing and instead simply holds onto the iron of the rail, cold metal that she wishes she could put back inside her spine, but she is unable to. She has the sensation that her body is collapsing.

"Sh, sh, sh…"

Now it is Frank holding her from behind—his body welcome; his body part of her body—but he is only softness and flesh, as she is. When he was a child, both of his parents were killed in the Indian Wars. Sometimes at night, he talks in his sleep and cries.

"Look what Mr. Edison has arranged for you," he says.

At the edge of the platform is a table covered by a huge gramophone. Next to it is a bottle of champagne and two long-stemmed glasses.

"Pour the champagne, Annie."

But she will not. She bends down and kisses the iron of the rail that is solid and real. She likes its taste, its smell, like the taste and smell of her gun or the taste of blood. How small she still is, like a girl running across the prairie. If Frank were not holding her, she would stand on the rail and fly away.

―――――――

"Terminus" is a work of fiction inspired by the life of Annie Oakley and the painting *Annah the Javanese* by Paul Gauguin, 1893, oil on canvas. Private Collection.

Still Life with Cherries

Her first memory is of the sun. It is Paris, she is two years old. She stands in her father's private courtyard, a small child with nut-brown hair and dark eyes, and looks up at the shining orb until it blinds her. She closes her eyes, feeling the warmth of the sun on her already tan skin, and when she opens them, sees spots that make her laugh. The spots go away. She looks up again at the trees.

If she could say the words, she would say, "This is the world."

She feels it reach out around her in complete safety, what she knows of the world outside the courtyard, and the people in the world, and the people in her life—mother, father, sisters, brother. It is a world full of love and trust and beauty, light sparkling down from above and the warmth of the shining yellow ball on her body.

She is sleepy. She lies down in the center of the private courtyard, curls up in a ball, and sleeps.

Much later her mother Veronique comes and picks her up, when it is growing dark. Louise rouses and cries, but quickly quiets, sensing her mother's breasts, their perfume. They sit in the chair before the fire and her mother opens her dress.

Veronique closes her eyes in this free time she has feeding her daughter. She strokes Louise's sweet head, her third daughter. The child's hair is already long. In birth, even, it covered her head, rich and dark. Next year she will end the nursing, as she is with child again. She is such a stubborn child. Louise's little fists will ball together, her face red with tears. Veronique secretly likes her stubbornness, admires it. It will help her endure life, she thinks.

She watches her husband Nicolas by the table, brooding over the accounts of the local artists' guild that he directs. His stature has increased their income, but also his labor. Paintings of other artists line their living quarters and seep into the courtyard. On market day, he and his apprentices maintain a stall where they sell the works of half the artists of Paris, but it is not a small task. When he is not worrying over guild matters, he is hard at work on his own still lifes or portraits. She has sat for him more than once in costumes meant to represent the court. He is a large man, his great beard halfway down his chest and black deacon's cloak that shrouds him, his manner serious and dark. She thinks of the young man he once was, with his hairless angular chin and blue eyes, and sees no resemblance. And perhaps he sees no resemblance in her, with her thick rolls of flesh and hooded eyes.

How does youth turn into this? she wonders, the bright promise so alive for an hour and then gone? She must not think such thoughts; God's gift of life is not some entertainment to be merely enjoyed. At night, though, he still lays his hand on her and she can feel the comfort of his life next to hers before she falls asleep. In the morning, he rises earlier than she does. When she comes to make the meal, he is kneeling in the courtyard, his eyes closed to God.

Louise sits at a table at the back of their church with three other girls copying words from the Bible, *and He stood and blessed the people and a light shone from His eyes*. Teacher comes and moves her hand so the letters will be more perfect. She likes the silence of the church, the sunlight from a high window and the plain dark wood of the pews, but the stone walls are cold. On Sundays they come here also—father, mother, sisters, brother—to listen as the man talks. Sit still, her mother whispers. Cross your hands. She tries, but it is difficult.

Today is for writing. She bends over the paper and carefully makes the letters. She is a girl though sometimes she wishes she were not. As a boy, she could stand with her father in the market and attend the regular school. She could run in the fields. Her body is made for running, not sitting as the women do at church, the light shining on their white collars. But she is lucky. Her father wants her to read and write, so she comes to the church with a few other girls and learns her letters.

He says that if she were Catholic, she would have no education, but she is Huguenot, not Catholic. Catholics kill you, her father says. They killed your uncle and his family. There is a hot poker in his voice when he says it, and she is afraid to look at his face. Once, she brought home a lump of Catholic incense that she'd found in the street—did not know what it was, thought it merely a piece of charcoal to draw with and imagined the pictures she would make to please him—and his face got so angry, spit coming from his mouth. "You are Huguenot!" he yelled, heat rising to his cheeks. She had never seen him so angry. It made her cry. He opened the door and threw it into the street. Much later he came and kissed her and said he was sorry, but still she cried.

She smells the soup warming on a fire at the back of the church and it makes her hungry. She tries to keep still, but her mind wanders. She likes to wander. If she were an insect, she would wander down the stone wall of the church and find the top of her own head. That's funny. She touches the top of her head, but there is no insect, and looks at the words again, the curve of each letter...*And He stood and blessed the people and a light shone from His eyes.* She likes the form of each letter and imagines herself an insect, riding them all. It makes her giggle.

After they eat, they draw—a cup and an apple—as her father does at home. Now she is serious like he is, though maybe it is just the silence that makes her serious. When she draws, the whole world is reduced to the scratch of her charcoal on the paper. This is her second favorite time of day, drawing. Sometimes it is enough just to stare at the apple and watch the sun carve a line across its bright stomach. Her favorite time is nighttime when she is allowed to crawl into bed with her mother and feel her warm body next to her own, smell her breath, and look into her eyes. Her mother is still nursing her youngest brother, and she lets Louise touch her breasts, feel their softness. Of all people on earth, she thinks her mother is the most wonderful.

She falls asleep that way each night. In the morning, her mother walks her into the cold Paris streets and back to the church. Sometimes, instead of the church, they go to the market with all the smells and food and noise. So much happens at the market. It is exciting but it also frightens her. Dead animals hang from ropes, flies buzzing, as huge men in bloody clothes slice pieces of the meat to sell, their faces laughing in the sun. The fruits and vegetables are quieter. She likes this part better, to let her fingers dribble across their fat, rosy bellies. Once a lady gave her a plum. Her lips touched the firm, purple skin, but when it broke, the juice ran over her chin and made her laugh. A dog trailed after them, lapping at what fell out of her hands. She had plum juice on her face all day until her mother wiped it off before the last meal. Later, before she slept, she gazed at a bowl of peaches on the table in a last sliver of light.

"Louise! Hurry!"
"No!"
She is bent over the plants, stroking them, talking to them, but her brother Bartholomew yanks her arm and pulls her into the street.

"Let me go!" Her hair falls from her bonnet, and she barely has time to retrieve it before he yanks her toward him, her feet flying.

He says he will take her to one of the loud places with grown-ups and musical instruments. Music that does not glorify God is forbidden. Each Sunday, the choir sings, but the stern music frightens her, echoing in the church against the black dresses and robes, the only color allowed them. Around their necks, the women must wear bleached white cowls to show their purity; though she is only half grown, she must wear one now too. It scratches her; she hates it. Her brother does not wear one.

"Let me go!" she cries, but he tugs too hard, with glistening eyes that refuse to listen. He pulls her beside the sweaty flanks of horses, their hard hooves stomping in mud and garbage. She wants to stop, but he yanks her arm so hard that she can almost feel it pull from her shoulder.

"Hurry, Louise, hurry!"

Why hurry? What game does he play? Bartholomew always plays games, even though their father forbids it: blind man's bluff in the alley with the other boys, or knights, where they ride each other and do battle, his red lips shining with saliva. Her father says he will come to nothing. Now the saliva nearly pours from them.

"Shh!" he commands, though she says nothing. They are

stopped outside the music place, drunken men and women falling through the door and onto the street. "Come!"

But inside there is little to see, above the ocean of dark legs, the shoes caked with dirt, and the white flesh of the women's thighs on the men's laps. This is where the people come who are not Huguenot, their mother says. She has told them about such places and that they must never go, so her brother has broken this rule as well. It is frightening to break rules, but also exciting. Something thrums in her chest from the broken rule and she forgets the danger, feeling only energy inside of her. She is so short that she can barely see over the tops of the tables.

She smells it, though, the sour soup of beer and animal and man, and then above, she hears the loud shouts that come from every corner. When she hears the music for the first time, the tinkling sounds enter her body and pierce her, better, even, than rainbows. Why has she not been allowed this till now, surely it is the voice of God just as color is his face? If she could, she would wear a yellow dress to honor God, or maybe one of rose. Color is the face of God. She peers up on her toes to see it.

"Look," her brother whispers, "that's a lute." He points to a man cradling a round wooden box with strings, and when the man plucks a string, music fills her. The other, Louise knows, is a recorder. They have one at home, though the music from this recorder is high and wild, weaving in and out of the lute and painting pictures.

All at once, a man sings the pictures. His song puts a dance in her heart, that makes her body move. Men and women around her move also, bodies swaying into each other. She closes her eyes and rides the wave of the music, fast and intricate, then light and fresh, like running through flowers. She can see the flowers, fields and fields of them, and feel herself fall into them.

Is it because her eyes are closed that she does not realize her father has entered the tavern, grasping them both by their collars and throwing them harshly into the street? His face is on fire.

"Never," he screams, "and in this filthy place!"

In the street the music is gone, just the shouts and sounds of animals and people. The field of daisies is gone, the sewage of the street cold and filthy. At home he forces them to kneel for hours in the courtyard to ask God's forgiveness, then puts them to bed without supper.

His anger does not live long, though. It never does. In the morning he strokes her cheek and serves her porridge, kissing the top of her head.

"I am sorry," he says, "for getting so angry." He keeps his face stern, but Louise can still see crinkles of love around his eyes. "But only God may live at the center of music. You must remember this. Promise me, Louise, never to go to such a place again."

There is yearning in his voice, even pain. She does not want to make the promise. Why must she deny herself this beauty? Isn't beauty also a part of God? Behind him out the window she can see the small red finch she likes to feed hop on the sill and wait for its food.

"I promise, Papa."

He lays his large hand on her head, so large that it covers her scalp and he nods.

Louise's hand moves expertly across the paper, carving the edge of the peach in charcoal, its pink-orange body in the center of the plate. She is dissatisfied with a line, looks carefully to find the fault, and begins again. "Observe," her father says in her mind. "Art is born from your observation of the world. The central lines are most important, but do not expect to find them quickly, for the secrets of nature reveal themselves slowly."

Yes, slowly, she must remember this. She takes a fresh sheet and begins again, studying the lines of the fruit and its soft shadows as her father instructed. He taught her so many things, how to mix color for him, prepare panels for his paintings, sketch compositions. A year before she was old enough, he made her his apprentice and took her to the countryside, where they drew trees and animals for hours as they picnicked on fruit and cheese.

She tries to hear more of his instruction, but cannot. He has been gone for three years, now, his fierce Huguenot eyes no longer piercing hers, but his arms also gone which held her so tightly. She does not want to think about his death, one night from a fever. They were all by his bedside, and in one moment, his soul left. After that, she felt no sun, and a wind blew through her life for a long time. She went into his courtyard, but his trees were dying because he was not there to love them. She cried against the trees and though her mother told her to come inside, she refused. Why could her mother not feel this emptiness? Paint the world black, she thought; stand immobile and do not breathe. If I do not breathe, perhaps he will come back, or I will die and then go to him. One day she tried to stop breathing, but she had not the courage to succeed. Not eating was easier. What was the reason for eating? She did not eat for two days.

"If you do not eat, Louise, you must stay in the courtyard," her mother said. Her voice was cold and she turned from her, though in truth, Veronique was not so much angry as greatly concerned. If Louise had been a baby, she would have fallen on the floor in a tantrum, she thought, her face red and obstinate. But she was too old for tantrums. Good food must not go to waste.

The courtyard was cold, a light snow beginning to fall, so she finally came inside and sat at the table. The smell of the food made her sick. She stared at her mother whose back was to her. Why could she not feel her father's loss as she did? She ate what she was forced to eat, but that was all, and each day after that, only the least required. Within days, she lost the flesh on her almost-grown body, and she was glad of it, to take her place closer to her father. When Veronique realized what she was doing, she yelled at her in earnest and called her "stubborn," but it made a secret happiness in Louise's heart to give him this sacrifice, to only eat the smallest amount and no more. Sometimes when no one was looking, she wrapped the food in her skirts and gave it to the dogs.

Now, months later, she grinds the colors for her stepfather Garnier and sketches his dull tableaux. In five or six years, she will begin her own master works, and when she finishes them, she will be no one's apprentice. Like her father before him, Garnier directs the artists' guild, but it is not the same. She does not admire his paintings—stilted, ugly canvases that capture nothing. Art for him is merely a living. As she draws, she thinks of the day she betrayed her father, to sit at her mother's table and put the food in her mouth and worse, to follow Garnier's orders, only months after he had died. She despises herself for the betrayal, but what choice did she have? She thinks of how her father stood, so tall and proud with his black and silver beard; she has put that inside of her, the way he stood. She is not tall, but she will stand tall. If she cannot grieve him, she will be like him, a true artist, who will capture the beauty of the world in truth and modesty. She has made that her promise to him and will keep it.

She sets down her charcoal and folds her hands over the full, black dress she now must wear, with a high ruffled collar because she is old enough. She must offer God her purity and chastity, above all her humility, to not set herself above others. The footstep of a woman, their deaconess says, must not bend a flower nor disturb the smallest insect. Such virtue no longer bothers her, because when she is silent, her mind is free, to fly outside the window or wherever she likes. Today it flies to God.

It is the darkness before rising, the world only a kernel of what it will be a few hours from now, before the raucous heat of midday, and each day God makes it anew. The cicadas are so loud and the morning birds, a brushstroke of light on the ceiling from the coming sunrise.

Though it's cold and she shares the bed with two of her sisters, Louise rises quietly and stands before the just open window, smelling deeply of the few stars still left, her hand on her belly, as she watches the morning sunrise. Though her belly is not much larger than yesterday and she is barely fifteen, she knows she is with child, and there is a terrible fear in her, for this law she has broken and for its consequence, but if she is truly honest, also an excitement: that just as God is creating a new day outside her window, she is creating a new life inside her body, from merely a thought in her eyes and in the boy's. Her mother does not know yet, no one does. On the day she tells her, she will stand tall and not look away. What she has done is beyond redemption; she knows this. She will surely be exiled from the community, but all sensations are sensations of God, are they not? And why, just because she is a girl, is her sinning greater than the boy's, merely because the evidence of it will appear on her body?

She met him at her friend Elsbeth's house. Elsbeth's mother prepared honey cake and tea for the small gathering. Of course he was Huguenot, all the boys were, studying at a nearby Academy.

She tried to swallow her thoughts, to only listen as was her duty, but she could not stop herself. He spoke of Francis Bacon. There were no old laws to understand, the boy said. Truth lived only in what one saw in the moment. "Once the idols are eliminated,'" he quoted, "'the mind is free to seek knowledge of natural laws."

"Yes, exactly," she said. "Knowledge is only found in a careful observation of the world!"

Her cheeks flushed red to have spoken. She fell back into silence, but the words could not be retrieved. There was no one at her school, now, of just a handful of girls continuing their studies, to talk to about such matters, and her teachers gave them nothing beyond Aquinas. She admired Aquinas' thoughts, but they were all to the purpose of discovering and upholding God's pre-ordained laws. This was entirely different, to learn life through observation, entirely anew. Embarrassed, she looked down at her hands folded neatly in her black skirt and squeezed them, but the boy smiled and touched her hand, putting great sensation in her body for her to observe.

More words fell out of her, ideas she had not spoken since she and her father would talk. They spoke in the courtyard sometimes at midday when the family slept, her father encouraging her mind though it was improper. He told her she had a great mind and could be a great painter if she so desired. The next day because the boy asked her, and most of all because she wanted it, they met, in the rooms of his older friend. She was clear what was happening throughout—that she would not see him again, and further, that such actions could easily bring her a baby. She did not think, then, of exile from the community; least of all, the proper behavior of girls. She knew, only, that her body and mind were equal to the boy's, her existence here on earth equal, and she had the right to sense what there was for her in this life and know it as she knew the peach on the tree or the morning sunrise outside her window. The mind must be set free to seek its own knowledge of natural laws, regardless of what others might say.

She did not see him again, and did not think she wanted to, until her monthly bleeding stopped. For a brief moment, an image of his yellow hair, woven through with marriage wreaths, crossed her mind, but she exiled it quickly. She would refuse to say his name, and even if she did, what good would it do? With the coming of summer, the boys, Elsbeth said, had left for their towns.

There are sounds in the kitchen. She must go down soon. Perhaps today she will tell Veronique. "Childbirth is dangerous," her mother will say. "You may die, and if that is God's punishment, it is just for such behavior."

But Louise is not afraid. She imagines her naked body out under the peach tree, next to the boy's naked body, bright sunlight all around, as she puts his hand where the baby is. "My belly is part of God and I am part of God," she says, "so even if I die, it will be God's death. I am not afraid."

She is not aware of the pain until it is on her, a deep, sharp gnawing in her back that goes on and on and will not stop. Vaguely, as though happening to some other person, her forehead is dampened, arms, she is given a dram of something to swallow. (She does not know this is all her mother, cradling her head and singing to her softly, sponging her, does not know of anyone's presence beyond the presence of pain.) A moment later the gnawing starts again, arms flailing, rags flying, a wild chaos around her and she has made it all. She hates the thing inside of her now because it is doing this to her. She sees it as a shiny, black, clawing thing. What does it have to do with her and the boy and the sweetness their bodies made together?

Once, Louise wakes. Her body is screaming, but she wakes. She sits halfway up in bed (or is it just a dream?) and listens as the churches ring somewhere far off in the city and a finch flies in the window and speaks in her ear. "I have come from God," it says. "Be silent. All this will be over soon. One of you will live and one will die. God chooses you." As the bird says *you*, it touches her cheek and flies out the window. She sees the tiny beak perfectly, yellow, like wood, and one small black eye.

All in a rush, the baby comes, the blood.

Later, her mother wakes her and shows her the tiny body before putting it in the ground. It came out wrong, she says, feet first, and then the cord was wrapped around its little neck. Louise was lucky she did not die.

She can see her mother has been crying, but she will not look at it, the pain thing. That's how she thinks of it. She snaps her head away, but still catches a sliver of face, the tiny sculpted mouth like Mary's baby in the paintings, a matting of hair above. She will not think of it. All she wants right now is to step into the heavenly ocean of no pain, no sensation, first one toe in the water, then the next, testing, unsure, will the gnawing start again or is it really over? Her back that was gnawed on, where is it? She moves a thumb around and is surprised to feel it there, unchanged, only damp against the bed.

She can feel hands around her putting her flesh into water, washing her. Slowly, slowly, each part of her body starts to relax, like walking into a warm lake until the water rises nearly above her head, steam rising around her and her body floating free.

Hours later she wakes in the clean bed with sunlight on her skin, and when she looks out the window and sees a bird, she wonders why God chose her. There must be a purpose, she thinks. She sees again the face and tuft of hair and then she sleeps. Veronique holds the infant to her chest, wondering if her beating heart might bring it back to life. She has never felt true anger for Louise until now, to have brought this to the family and most of all to this innocent life. There is so much stubbornness and sin in her. The elders will gather to discuss her disgrace, and if Louise is sent from the community, she will grieve but she will not disagree.

Veronique digs the grave herself in the courtyard and lays the baby inside. Emily she will call her. Every person on this earth deserves a name and maybe for a moment Emily breathed air before she died. That is a life and a lifespan, if only for one moment. She cannot stop crying for her.

As the days pass, Louise heals. She lies under a pomegranate tree in the sun. Her older sister Naomi cooks large stews to recover her health and her stepfather Garnier brings her paper to draw. There will be a fair soon, he says, eager for the money she can make with her skillful hand, but when she lifts the charcoal, she can only draw the baby.

The air around Louise is silent as she begins the new work. She puts a blue cloth on the table that she will use for the still life and in its center, a blue porcelain bowl. She tumbles a mound of cherries, still warm from the market, into the bowl and behind it, a smaller bowl of gooseberries. These will be at the center of the picture, but the still life is not yet right. What else is required?

A painting must be more than simply the creation of a pleasant image. There must be a purpose behind it though she is not yet able to put that into words. The experience of the baby has changed her, and she knows it will change her painting as well. She understands now that she was wrong to do such a thing. It is true that the evidence of the sin did not adhere to the boy's body as it did hers, and so the burden of blame was unfair, but that is the nature of a woman's body. It collects the consequence, and in this she agrees with her mother, though little else.

Each day, now, they raise their voices to each other, as though there is no longer love between them. This morning Veronique told her that the church elders will not shun her, but require a rapid marriage. A much older widower has been found. When Veronique mentioned the church and the widower, Louise's back stiffened, her mind shut to all discussion. What right had the elders to say how she must live?

She did not answer and instead showed her mother the angular line of her shoulders and the swift movement of her body around the kitchen, as though the words just uttered carried no weight.

Veronique watched for several moments, remembering the stubbornness of Nicolas and now the same passed on to this daughter. "There will come a time when I will die and Garnier will remarry, and then this house and all of its belongings will pass to him and his new wife who will not want you. Or he will die and this house and all of its belongings will pass to his son and his bride. You play too loosely with your future, Louise. You are young but will not always be so. Your shelter and even the food in your mouth exist only by God's grace."

Louise shut out her words. A part of her still wanted to climb into her mother's lap, but now there was only space between them.

She poured her tea. "You say nothing I do not know, Mother."

She left the room quickly and climbed the stairs to the attic of the house, rising above everyone. Only here can she truly breathe.

That was this morning. Now she stares at the still life of cherries, wondering what is wrong and refuses to think about her mother again. She stands to open the windows and smell the fresh air of the day. What a good space this is: fifteen paces wide, with windows front and back and clean, boarded floors; it will more than suffice for her plan. It took her and the girl a week to clear it of ancient furniture, but now that they have, how good to simply stand here, open to the light.

She closes her eyes and feels the morning reach around her. Unlike her brothers and sisters, she will never marry nor bear children beyond the single infant. Her paintings will be her children. And how is that wrong or less of an honoring of God, simply because of her gender? As she thinks of God now, the presence above her and out of her vision, it comes to her that this God whom she will honor must grant her something in exchange for her promise of chastity—never to experience such pain again, of her body or of her mind. She lights a candle and drops sharply to her knees, the vow unspoken but clear in her mind. In a year, she will complete her apprenticeship and become a master. Then she will use her gift in the service of art as her stepfather Garnier and others want, but in exchange, she must be granted a life free of pain. She knows it is blasphemy to make such an agreement with God, and in addition, a life without pain does not exist, but she does not care. This is her requirement. She promises God this as nuns do, if he will grant her the painting without pain.

If the bird flies in the window, she thinks, God has answered me and agreed. She stands and waits, only silence blowing into the room from the thin blue sky outside. And then it appears, the same small finch, with the yellow beak and bright blue wings. Like some kind of rare jewel, it is, this message from God. Unafraid, it flies back and forth through the garret, finds an open window, and flies away.

So, it is decided. She turns back to the cherries and gooseberries and tries to understand the missing element. There is the illusion of life that the artist creates, but behind it must rest a portion of actual life, that must be real and sincere. Thinking of the bird and the vow, it comes to her that the color of the cloth must contain both yellow and blue, to match the yellow and blue of the bird and so honor it. She will be the only one who knows this, but it is enough. She places a second, yellow shawl over the blue one, feels the rightness of the composition, and begins.

Inspired by the painting *Still Life with Cherries, Strawberries and Gooseberries* by Louise Moillon, 1630, oil on panel. The Norton Simon Museum. Pasadena, California.

Roman Glass

It was the dishwasher's hands Ruth noticed first. She did not know his name then, did not care to know it, only registered the flat, platypus fingernails as he operated the cafeteria's coffee urn, or the twitch of his arm muscles beneath his uniform as he carried a tray of dishes.

He appeared at the small Brooklyn museum in late November. She was pushing her tray along, taking the cafeteria's offerings for the day and thinking of nothing beyond this or that art collection and why it was important: Etruscan coins, Venetian earrings, a group of Titian paintings, each with its own story. Her specialty was the history of collecting. She and a few other curators had invented it—the idea that the patronage of the church, or of kings and billionaires, was as important as the artwork itself, since after all, it was their support that had saved the artifacts or made the paintings possible. To value and be valued was key. Her father, a retired medievalist from Columbia University, said what people collected was irrelevant and to prove it, had given away most of his possessions to Goodwill when he moved to a senior citizens home in New Jersey. She visited him every Sunday and he invariably brought up the topic—why the history of collecting was a meaningless pursuit, even though she'd built her career on it and was now herself lecturing at Columbia on the topic. He spoke from a large, brown recliner which looked out on a sun-drenched patio, an oxygen tank nearby, and said that the things people accumulated in their lives, even relationships, were mere accident and it was digressionary to think otherwise. Her birth was an accident, he would announce in a crescendo of logic, since if a different sperm and egg had met inside her mother, she herself would not exist. He never regarded her as he spoke, as he had rarely looked at her throughout her childhood.

She would patiently counter that the first collector had been Noah, and if he had not built his ark, none of them would exist. Yes, it was just a story, but the Bible itself made the point. Her father was unmoved. Sometimes when they spoke, she imagined her words hovering in the air above him, waiting for a recognition that never came, and in the parking lot afterwards, dizzy and disoriented, she was unable to recognize her car from the scores of other compact models, lined up as though on a car lot. He had been a young man at Auschwitz, which more than one psychiatrist said accounted for his detachment, but the explanation never comforted her. Only returning to the museum office could orient her again, and to the careful charts she and others had made to show the influence of this or that Medici's taste on the history of art—proof that what people chose to include in their lives did matter.

"When did you first notice me?" she asked, lying in the dishwasher's arms. His name was Juan Estrada, but she preferred the dishwasher. That's how she described him to herself. It was a Sunday morning, a late January snow drifting down on the sidewalk outside, but it was warm in his Queens apartment, and warmer still in his bed.

He stroked her face gently, kissing her eyelids. "I always noticed you. You were a bird. Put that woman in a cage with my birds. That's what I thought."

The dishwasher spoke like a poet, which was no accident. Before spending ten years in prison on a bad drug charge, he had been a high school Spanish teacher who wrote poetry on his days off and did his thesis on Pablo Neruda. Now no school would have him. One day he would write poetry again, he said, maybe when she went with him to San Juan to meet his family or at least to his sister's apartment in Coney Island, where he had dinner each Sunday. He had put his sister's address in Ruth's purse that morning and repeated again that she should come; it would be his nephew's birthday. He spoke frequently about San Juan, the blue of the ocean that met the fragile pink beaches, and how he longed to take her there. He kept a small aviary of finches in his cheap Queens apartment, but his sheets were always clean for her, the yellow light from the window spilling across them now, making her think they were already on the pink sand.

He moved his body over her and she could feel him get hard again. It was mid-morning and she should leave, but she did not want to. She was fifteen years older, but he said he liked it that way. Their affair had been going for three months, and though she intended to end it, there was never a right time.

He put himself inside her, and they began to make love. "What made you see me?" "It was your blue suit," he said softly into her neck. "It matched your eyes." And she had seen his hands, stroking the coffee machine gently, the way he stroked her now. When they finished, he made her the Puerto Rican coffee she loved and they ate pan dulce, sitting at his small table by the window. He opened one of his many poetry books and read a poem by an obscure Bolivian poet, first in Spanish, then in English: "I had no one before you," he recited. "You rose me up / Your face at the window / Tears as large as jewels falling from your eyes / My childhood is forgotten in your arms."

The beauty of the poem stayed with Ruth all morning, the truth it evoked, of that kind of sadness healed by that kind of love. Before she left, he asked her again to come to his sister's, and she could see it was important to him. Meeting relatives, being introduced as his girlfriend, though, was not something she was ready for. She said she would try.

By the time she pulled into the parking lot of her father's retirement home, it was afternoon, the snow melted in the winter sun, and though the words were gone, the feeling of the poem made Ruth more aware of the moment the crisp air and tall pines that surrounded the building. Sunny Pines was an hour outside of Manhattan, and though a long drive, she always appreciated the small forest of trees that greeted her, like Thomas Mann's mountain resort in Switzerland, she thought, the first time she saw it. She sat for several moments at one of the picnic tables that edged the forest, a community area for the warmer months, and tilted her head back as far as she could to see the branches of snow-covered trees that reached into the sky. Trees collected nutrients in their roots to see them through the winter, but what had she collected in her life? Thanks to her job, she had been able to purchase a small apartment in Park Slope when prices were reasonable, and fix it up with some decent furniture. Nowadays, though, it just looked cramped and dusty to her, barely worth the cleaning lady who came twice a month. It was only her collection of Roman glass from the third century that was important, and that she had managed to buy over the years at auction. The small pieces were slightly damaged or considered less important, so in her price range.

She displayed the lavender and pink objects near a window that looked out onto a neglected backyard. Since she rarely had visitors, only she saw them, which is how she liked it. She would kneel next to the pieces at eye level to better appreciate their ripples and iridescence in the light from the window—small fragilities too delicate to show the world.

"Father?"

At first Ruth did not realize his room was empty. She was about to start talking when she turned and saw his stripped bed, with no sign of occupancy.

A deep fear shot through her. She went into the hall to find a nurse to yell at for changing his room without notifying her. She refused to consider anything worse. Besides, when residents died or were hospitalized, Sunny Pines was obligated to contact next of kin. It is true his health had been failing, congestive heart failure with its risk of stroke now added to his list of ailments, and since she was his legal guardian, his doctors had encouraged her to sign a DNR for him, a do-not-resuscitate order, should he have a medical crisis. The thought of her father in some hideous state and hooked up to machines was not a vision she wanted to contemplate, and he had agreed. They discussed it a few months before, or rather she did, as was their custom. He lay in bed staring at a cloud out the window and mumbling in answer to her questions and comments. Frustrated, she had stood between him and the window so he was forced to look at her, and said she needed an affirmative answer, that "yes," he agreed to the DNR.

"Yes," he said, in a surprisingly clear voice.

"I will be here and so will the nurses. You will not be alone."

She squeezed his hand and he squeezed hers back. His blue-gray eyes seemed to open to her and it made her think of the young man he must have been in the concentration camp, not more than fifteen or sixteen. Toward the end of the war, he had organized an escape with five or six other young men, and they actually made it, hiding out in the dead of winter in Poland, eating God knows what; then after the war he made his way to Israel where he met her mother, before they came to the U.S. As a teenager, Ruth would stare for hours at an old passport photo of him from the time, a broad-shouldered young man with wavy dark hair and glistening eyes, wondering how that person had become her father. Her mother had died of breast cancer when Ruth was sixteen, and that was what changed him for good. She and her father stood at the gravesite, Ruth adrift and broken-hearted and her father barely able to hold her hand. Hunched in a long overcoat, he looked like a painting by Goya, brooding and entirely hidden.

She caught sight of her father at the end of the corridor being wheeled back to the room, his usual expression at seeing her, or rather non-expression, on his face.

"A little accident," the nurse mouthed to her. "We had a nice bath, didn't we?" she said in her father's ear. His hearing was also failing.

He made a face. "Hello, Father." He glanced at Ruth and turned away. While an orderly put on clean sheets, she asked her regular questions of how his week had been and whether he wanted anything special from the city for their visit next week.

Their conversation was as it usually was, Ruth doing most of the talking, her father falling asleep as soon as he was back in his bed.

"The orderly made a mistake and didn't put on diapers after his bath," the nurse explained to Ruth in the corridor. "It won't happen again."

Ruth did not go to dinner in Coney Island, did not even think of it, until she saw the dishwasher in the cafeteria on Monday morning. He shrugged and looked at her with a mixture of pleasure to see her, disappointment, and acceptance.

He was a fatalist where love was concerned, he told her once. You got that way in prison out of necessity. He did not believe in broken hearts. She liked that, his consistency, knowing he would be there for her, and at the same time asking little of her. She wondered how long it would last.

The first week of February, the museum was more crowded than usual, their gift shop holding its annual sale. In addition, visitors were there for an exhibit of Jackie Kennedy's suits that a woman on Fifth Avenue had assiduously collected and then left to the museum. Most of the suits were Chanel originals in pastel colors of Angora wool and silk, and the show's curator had dressed the mannequins in matching platform heels and earrings. Inside, tapes of singers like Frank Sinatra and Perry Como played at very low volume, perfectly evoking the intelligence and chic of the First Lady when her husband was in office.

Ruth had seen the show when it first opened, but stepped into the gallery at the end of her lunch hour to enjoy it again. People called the period Camelot, and then the end of Camelot when the president was assassinated. It was well before she was born, but she had studied it in school, and met the collector opening night. Greta Epstein was an immaculately dressed woman in her mid-eighties, her father's age, but with the grace of someone much younger. The suit she wore was from the period, in a deep rose pink, with matching shoes and stockings.

Ruth asked questions about her collection, who her favorite designers were and what other objects she owned. She told Mrs. Epstein about her specialty, the history of collecting, and why the influence of one collector could be so important. They could bring the past to life, like Mrs. Epstein's had.

"Of course, it's not a pleasant thought, but these suits make me think of Dealey Plaza," Ruth said, "and the suit Jackie wore that day. Do you know where it is?"

"It's in the National Archives," Mrs. Epstein answered in a low voice. "It will never be put on public display, but they keep it for historical reasons."

Now as Ruth wandered the exhibit alone, she thought again of the blood-stained suit, and how the First Lady had kept it on the entire day of the shooting, so the cameras would see and record it. The Zapruder film also played in her mind, of that hopeful motorcade, and then the fateful bullets and the First Lady leaning out the back of the car, the president's shot-out brains on the seat next to her. Ruth had watched different versions of it for the class at school, in slow motion, fast motion, with different enhancements, frame by frame. For years frame 313 of his head exploding had been kept out of it, too gruesome, Zapruder said, to show the world, but by the time she was in school, all the gunshots were in: the first, catching him in the throat, Jackie turning to tend to him, and then the fatal one, with the puff of smoke cutting his head in two. Seconds later, Jackie was out the rear of the car in the pink, blood-drenched suit, escaping, some said when they first saw the film, but that wasn't true; she was reaching for the forensic evidence, the piece of his skull blasted away, grabbing for it as though she could put him back together.

February passed quietly at the museum, then March. By the middle of April, the rows of the museum's renown yellow tulips had appeared in the museum garden, poking their heads through the soil. Ruth and the dishwasher continued their liaison—that was a better word for it than relationship, Ruth decided—though on some weekends she was gone on business trips or he at a chef certification class he was taking at a local college.

She had yet to visit his sister's in Coney Island, and he had stopped asking her. Her father's health remained stable. The regularity of her life was what so pleased Ruth, like the regularity of the seasons—moments of excitement limited to when she might read an interesting article in one of the journals about this or that collector, or an important idea she might have about an artist.

Nearing fifty-five, her time of great love affairs and revolutions was over, and she was glad of it. Life was to be looked back upon, like art history. As the philosopher Kierkegaard said, while life was lived forward, it could only be remembered backward, and she much preferred the backward glance.

She ran her hand over the internal memo listing the upcoming openings for the following six months: household silver of Czar Nicholas' court at the time of the Revolution; Picasso's ceramic works; second and third century glass techniques. That time was wracked by civil war and conflict, and yet it had produced arguably the most beautiful artifacts of the Roman era. Her pieces were not important enough to be shown, but she would contribute an article.

The call came in from Sunny Pines about a half hour before the end of the day. Her father had suffered a serious coronary incident. Because of his DNR, they were not sending him to the hospital.

When she arrived in the early evening, he was in a coma, his eyes open but unseeing, grayed over, his mouth open. His face was turned toward a window, and though she knew this was unlikely, he looked happy, as though he were encountering someone he had not seen in a long time. She hoped it was her mother.

The nurse said it could take anywhere from two to six hours for the death process, probably not longer. She advised Ruth to sit with him and hold his hand, talk or sing to him; that hearing was the last sense to go. Periodically, an orderly came in to give him drops of morphine in his mouth, in case he was in pain.

She picked up his hand and felt his whole body tremble, as though he were trying to rouse himself to consciousness to say something.

"I'm here, Daddy," she said, whispering in his ear. She stroked the silver hairs on his forehead and kissed him. "I love you so much. I promise, I won't leave you! I'm here."

She cradled his head and kissed his forehead, humming to him, trying to think of a song he would like. As a young man, he had been a wonderful singer, a relative told her. In Germany where he grew up, he had started a collection of old Yiddish folk songs before the Nazis came. All that was lost, but sometimes he would sing at night in the camps, his voice rising through the silence, and people called him the Singer. "Will the Singer sing tonight?" they would whisper. He had to be very careful. He could be badly punished, even killed if a guard found out; to give that kind of solace to a broken heart.

What songs did she know? What had he sung to her? A scrap of something in Yiddish came to her, from when she was five or six, laughing on his knee and staring at the sunlight out the window—a lilting melody in a minor key of a boy who dreams of being a bird and flies to heaven, and she hummed it to him now, picturing the young man in the photograph—all that hope and promise we carry inside of us until history takes it away.

A hospice nurse came in and began to stroke his feet.

"It's started," she said. "The bluing of the cardiovascular system—do you see?—the blood rushes to the feet, then back up and down again. It will be about thirty minutes now."

The nurse positioned herself at her father's feet and lightly held them as Ruth cradled his head and continued to sing—louder now, unself-conscious, of the boy and the bird. She saw the boy-bird in her mind taking off across the sky, and just as she did, her father's breathing became labored, then stopped. Just like that, it stopped.

She looked at the nurse, who nodded.

In a rush, her love for him came to her, the intensity of running into his arms as a five-year-old, the rock he was for her, and for a few minutes as she sobbed, she was that child again, fully a part of her father as he was of her, before their lives happened, before his great sadness that had driven them apart.

The rest of the day was consumed with waiting for the mortuary and paperwork, her father's empty body in the bed but unimportant. The funeral would be in three days per Jewish tradition, though there were few people to invite—maybe some old colleagues from Columbia, a neighbor or two, a few old relatives in the Bronx.

When she finally got back to her apartment in Park Slope, it was night of the following day, her cat whom she'd forgotten crying at her legs and desperate for food. She fed her quickly and got into bed. It had been two days now since she slept, and though she was exhausted, her eyes were wide open and she knew she was a long way from sleep. When she closed her eyes, she saw a jumble of images—paintings by Goya, Jackie Kennedy's bloody suit, her father's body—her ears buzzing. She got up, made herself some herb tea and took a sleeping pill. Only with difficulty did she drift off.

In the days and weeks that followed, Ruth set about composing a new life. Her father had always worn gold spectacles, and when the doctor prescribed reading glasses, she got herself a pair, stepping into her father's academic persona with flair. She gave a keynote address at a museum conference on her specialty, speaking with authority and ease, and without the nerves she usually got at such events. Nearing the end of her adjunct contract at Columbia, the chair invited her to submit for the tenured position that would be opening up in the fall, implying she had a good chance. For an interview with the hiring committee, she bought herself two new suits, unsure which to wear since they both gave her flair mixed with professionalism and grace, and besides, she would need them for the professorship she was sure she would get.

She was only sad that she had to break it off with the dishwasher, who had just been promoted to assistant of Kitchen Services. They met in the cafeteria one afternoon when it was quiet and both had free time, and she told him she was too busy, which was only partly true. She had begun dating a physics professor she'd met on OK Cupid who was older and "more appropriate," she told herself, though sometimes he bored her, and he did not please her as much in bed.

When she said it, he stroked his coffee cup, his sad eyes looking down and away, but said it was all right, he understood.

When he could, regardless of the season, the dishwasher went to Coney Island, in summer to fish and gaze across the ocean as though looking for Puerto Rico, and in winter, to sit in the warm, steamy coffee shops on the boardwalk, reading his poetry books and occasionally trying to pen one of his own. He had taken Ruth a few times to his favorite spots—life guard stations near the water or coffee shops on the boardwalk. At the time, Coney Island wasn't to her taste—the smell of corn dogs on sticks, the merry-go-rounds. Too much tinsel and noise, but on a Sunday morning in early May, Ruth woke up and without too much thought, threw on a pair jeans and a sweatshirt, her suit underneath, ate something quickly, and headed out on the subway. She had recently broken it off with the

OK Cupid physics professor, but that wasn't the real reason. There was something about the light outside her Brooklyn window and the desire to smell the ocean again.

She called and texted him several times, and, when he didn't answer, remembered what he had told her, that he liked to turn off his phone when he went to the beach, to feel more like a kid again, before cell phones which was before he went to prison. It wasn't hard to figure out where he'd be.

There had been a rainstorm at five or six in the morning that only lasted a few hours but seemed to wash everything clean. Not yet warm, Ruth nursed a cup of coffee on the boardwalk, then started out across the sand. Juan—she no longer wanted to call him the dishwasher, or even Johnny, what they called him in the kitchen, but his given name and his name as a poet, Juan Estrada, the person she could see him becoming one day.

The waves were green and blustery, foam and seaweed crashing on the shore. It made Ruth think of Christopher Columbus who had come from the Old World to Puerto Rico in just this weather, bringing his ships and soldiers to kill and be killed, so much violence, and all to spread Europe on a new continent. She spotted him standing near a life guard station.

As she walked across the sand to him, she felt different—less composed, emergent.

A couple of crazy kids in wet suits walked past her and down to the shore with their surfboards. When she was about twenty feet away, he saw her and waited, an open look on his face.

"I thought you might be here," she said.

"I am." He looked down at her and smiled. Ruth was a small woman, and in her sweatshirt and jeans, she looked almost like a child.

"I've been thinking about what I said." She paused. "I was wrong. I don't want to end it."

He stroked her cheek lightly. "I'm glad."

"Here, I brought you something." She dug in her jeans and took out a small fragment of pink glass, not more than half an inch long. On one end was a little hole and she had threaded a chain through it, so it was a kind of jewelry.

"It's Roman," she said. "From the third century." He held it up to the light.

"It's beautiful. Thank you." He put the chain around his neck, kissing her lightly on the cheek, and the scent of him brought back their Sunday mornings in his Queens apartment and all the ways she had missed him.

Ruth put her arm through his and they watched the surfers for a while, paddling out now, Ruth hoped not too far, but kids liked to do that, test themselves against nature. She told him she wanted to go to his sister's for lunch and they were going to leave, but they didn't. Instead they began collecting shells, showing each other their finds, becoming increasingly excited like children. For something to do with the shells, they constructed a small mountain of sand and embedded it with the shells, enlarged the mountain, embedded more. The surfers came back in, their wet suits dripping with seawater and perspiration, and when they saw the shell mountain, they pitched in, their wet bodies adding the scent of the ocean.

To Ruth, the shells brought to mind the face of the ocean and the unknown, and how many sailors had gone down in that sea. Stories came to her, great books of those crossings that she had read, and then other stories, of wars on the island with indigenous people, along with the wars of the second and third centuries in Rome when the Empire had almost fallen and when her glass was made. The primary component of Roman glass was common beach sand, no different from what she touched now, itself composed of tiny shells.

It was getting warm on the beach. She pulled off her sweatshirt to her bathing suit top, rubbed on some sun screen, and went back to gathering shells.

The museum in "Roman Glass" is fictional, but there are many examples of Roman glass around the world, including those at the Metropolitan Museum of Art in New York, the British Museum in London, and the Hermitage Museum in St. Petersburg, Russia.

Women Bathing

I

It is Renoir's newest paintings at the Luxembourg that give Marie the idea for her own work, his soft impressionistic images of women at their baths. She stares at one in particular, *Women Bathing*, scribbling notes with the stub of a pencil she holds tightly in her gloved hand. The metal basin barely reaches the ankles of the women, their thighs large and pastel in the center of the composition, painted in shades of the finest lavender and yellow. Across one woman's back is a filmy white towel mixing with the broad, ephemeral flesh, but the front of the body is barely visible. Why, Marie writes in her notebook. Why is only the muted flesh of interest to Renoir—the dull opacity of it? It is the same in the Degas painting hanging beside it, the breasts of his model positioned away from the viewer's eye, though here the interest is line and form, more than flesh.

Marie turns to a noise at the front of the gallery, a cluster of young men in black jackets and top hats, girls like pastel flowers gliding beside them, their parasols tucked under their arms. At the sound of the laughter, she instinctively turns away, shrinking inside her high-collared black dress, a size too large and stained with daubs of paint, but there is nothing she can do, it is the only one she owns. Gratefully few people notice her, with her slight frame and dull hair pinned tightly behind her ears. She sees one young man from Gleyre's studio, but barely nods when he catches her eye. In a moment, the group has passed to another room, chatting in excited whispers, and she has the gallery to herself, the strokes of light and color that fill her and make her heart beat. She sits on a bench, her skirts billowing, the skylight from the top of the museum pouring down on her and surrounding her in color. She wishes the color were inside of her instead of just in the sunlight. She closes her eyes in the bath of color, almost smelling it.

Soon she must leave. She studies the Renoir again, the idealized flesh of the model, and begins a sketch. The painting she will make will be so different, alive with everything she knows and has studied. Once, when Marie was younger and first knew she wanted be an artist, she had stripped nude and sat before her mother's looking glass for an afternoon to draw her own body because she had no other model, her half-formed breasts, female hair, and the space in between that covered what was inside of her.

She thinks about that afternoon in front of the looking glass, how different the feeling had been from Renoir's, with the prickliness of her hair and odor of her body mixing with the smell of the charcoal and paper. Outside her father's fields were hot, yellow. He would have been driving the oxen, her brothers next to him at their labor. If someone had caught her she would have been whipped, but none of that mattered. The truth was far too urgent, to describe every line of the stomach, the curve just so to the top of her leg.

At Gleyre's, they also have models—just the other day, in fact, a man. The place is well known because so many of them studied there: Monet, Renoir, Pissarro, talking into the night about the art they were creating that would change everything; now decades later, it is still surprising to Marie that she gained admittance. Paris is bursting with young people of both genders who want to be writers and artists, from abroad or simply the countryside like she is. They cluster in groups outside cafés, or walk arm in arm in museums. She is among them and at the same time not, standing apart. She tells herself it is because she is serious and studies more intently. There is so much to learn, but the truth is, she wants to be alone. Her first day at Gleyre's, she'd never drawn a man's body like that, exposed and in the light, and her hands shook from the newness of it, but also the maturity—that she was a real artist now, and the description of the human body was her primary job.

She closes her sketchbook, puts her pencil in her skirt, and leaves the small museum for the Paris streets, alive with carriages and parasoled women, horses stomping in the chilled air. The winter was difficult and the last snows have finally melted. She is ready to cross the boulevard when a motorcar rounds the corner and comes toward her, a shiny insect in the spring air. She still gasps when she sees them, more and more each day. People say there are over three thousand in Paris. The city is transforming before her eyes—a new metro, boulevards broadened and lined with trees, parks and squares renovated. Sometimes when she looks at Paris, it's as though she can touch the change, the new world that is coming to all of them. It frightens her and excites her in equal measure, and at the same time she knows that a real artist must *see* everything. Above all else, there must be no fear.

The African is laughing loudly when she walks into Gleyre's, drawings under her arm, to take her usual place at the back.

"Hello my Little One. Come, talk to us! Don't scurry off like a mouse."

Like her the African is an alien, someone who stands apart. Most at Gleyre's are privileged young men, with a girl or two scattered among them. She does not feel she can approach the girls, with their chattiness and flirtations. The African stands proudly in his Moroccan robes, his coal-black face grinning at her. She has heard that he models in his robes for Renoir, and that he is a favorite. When he opens his mouth, his teeth are so white, his head thrown back like a lion.

"Come, show us your drawings!"

Marie can't tell if he is being serious, or simply making fun of her as she knows others do. The students next to him turn to glance at her. Near the African, she is less timid. His long fingers are covered in rings, his enormous leg propped on a bench. While everyone at the studio including Marie dresses in black, his robes dazzle in every color of the rainbow.

"We are all students here!" he says. "Do not be afraid."

She turns to him, smelling cinnamon, and other fragrances she can't identify. "I am not afraid." She looks straight into his face to prove it, but it is not true; she is afraid of too many things: poverty, her loneliness, above all failing at her goal of becoming an artist. She would paint him with blue-black and vermillion, a touch of gold. She is close enough to see his ceremonial scars that rib his face in fantastic patterns.

"Show me your work," he commands, looking at the bundle of drawings under her arm.

"After," she says, swirling her skirts past him to take her usual place at the back. She has no interest in the comments of the other two—gentlemen artists, dabblers, they call them—boys who buy their way into the studios while awaiting an inheritance or a position in the family firm. The African is different; he has skill. She has seen enough of his drawings to know this. She would like to absorb his ability of pride and arrogance, to hold his head so high regardless of what others say. One day soon, she will show him her drawings and will look at his.

Just as she has set out her materials, Gleyre arrives, to lecture them on their job as artists and set the first pose. By now he is a foolish figure of a man in his artist's smock and dabbled palette, but his studio has seen too much fame to dismiss him. Slowly the room quiets as people work, charcoal scratching on paper. One or two young men light pipes; a few drink from silver flasks or throw long scarves over their shoulders and scrabble intently. Marie pins up a fresh sheet of paper, but her hand shakes so that she ruins her first two drawings, and only manages one decent one before the session is over. Why has the African upset her? She is an independent woman, is she not, who has been to the slaughter houses to draw the heads of dead pigs and knows how to navigate the streets of Paris at night?

At the end of the morning, she manages to escape without the African coming after her, but walking through a public garden toward her rooms, she sees him again, and this time forces herself not to run when he draws near.

They are just under a broad avenue of linden trees, their rich, white blossoms dropping from above like snow. It seems to Marie that when the linden trees bloom, all of Paris is pervaded by their scent. She lets him walk next to her, like all the other couples and families out for an afternoon stroll, but they are not like any of the other couples—she small and transparent with her straw-colored hair, he a fantastic African prince. Surely people must gawk.

At first they walk in silence, before he abruptly cries out, "What is your name!" making her start.

She turns to face him.

"What is your name?" he says again, his voice softer this time, his face strained.

"Marie Clouseau," she speaks in barely a whisper. She uses her father's name. She has not used her married name since the day she arrived in Paris.

He grins. "Abdul Nadir. How do you do?" He holds out his hand to shake, huge and calloused but gentle.

They continue in silence, under the arbor of trees that wrap them in their sweet, haunting fragrance. It is not the silence of shyness, she decides, but rather how important dignitaries must walk in Africa, gracing each other with their presence. Without warning, he sweeps his arm above his head, to the blossoms above them. "Look how fantastic they are! I am sad, that beauty exists like this and I am not yet strong enough to paint it. I will never be strong enough because I am not God."

She stops and turns to him. She is not sure how she finds the words, but they come from the deepest part of her. "Only God is God," she says. "But we are artists for a purpose. Monet's painting of the linden trees is certainly good enough, the new one from his window at Giverny. Have you seen it? One day you will make a fine painting of linden trees if you continue studying and do not give up hope."

He smiles, the glow on his face rising like the sun. "Of course. You are right. I thank you for reminding me, Mademoiselle Clouseau. You have the true heart of an artist." He touches her hand that is so small and white in his huge black one that it looks to her like a fantastic dove flying through a starry night.

"Goodbye Marie Clouseau," he says, removing his hat and bowing to the ground. "We are friends."

That night Marie starts a fresh page in her journal to describe the African, a fellow artist she calls him. He is so foreign as to make her feel that she has entered an entirely new world. She is not attracted to him, but there is something else here equally important.

Physical desire, she knows that feeling from her husband René, whose grave she has run from. And if he had not died, how different her life would be today—no Paris, no painting, only knowing heaven through another person's soul. She will not think about that now. Pain like that must not be remembered.

Besides, the feeling with Abdul is different, like entering possibility and growth. For a moment, she sees herself next to him in Africa, painting pictures of the great savannahs, hot and yellow. Giraffe lope beneath burning suns; lions nap under baobab trees.

But she is not in Africa and baobab trees do not grow in Algiers, where she has heard he is from. She looks around her room that has just enough space for a bed, a table, her easel, and a small closet for clothing and art supplies. She thinks again of her idea for a painting of the female body, an answer to Renoir, to show the truth of what she knows about being a woman. But where will she find the money to hire a model? What she told the African about study and hope is true, but it is difficult to always believe.

She lies back on her pillow. There was never a time she did not want to be an artist. It is so difficult, though. She has been in Paris three years and her life is hardly different than when she first arrived. She works as an artist's model to pay for Gleyre's, food, the rent of the small room. Of course she is out of her mind and in addition, the most pitiful of women, twenty-eight and alone. She knows she has talent, though it is not enough, and at the same time, there is no other life she can imagine.

II

Gleyre looks more shrunken today, from too many years painting bad landscapes in the sun, Marie decides, his skin wrinkled, stretched too tightly across his bald pate. But who is to say he is not a great artist, merely unrecognized in his lifetime? The Dutch painter Vermeer lived a lifetime with only modest recognition, and today his works hang in the Louvre. Behind Gleyre students trickle in: boys in dramatic coats with long cigarette holders; one, even, with a pet rat on a leash, draped around his neck! They are not only French but German, English, American, copies of Rimbaud in their pockets and full of talk of the clubs from the night before, where young girls dance with skirts raised high above their heads.

Before she has a chance to arrange her easel, Gleyre catches her shoulder: "Monsieur Renoir has asked me to find a model, and I thought of you," he whispers. "He would not object to a model of your appearance, and you would learn from him. You have talent. Of course he must meet you first. If the work is for a new painting, it could continue for some time."

At the mention of Renoir's name, a happiness blooms inside of her that is hard to contain. She will be able to get supplies for the painting, a larger room, more food. There are other girls in the studio, and he has asked her.

He looks at her clothes. "Do you own a different dress?"

"No."

"It does not matter. Wear your hair down with perhaps a flower. You are the only one I am sending."

"Thank you," she nods, sitting at her easel. She is hardly beautiful anymore, she knows this; has he taken pity on her or recognized her ability? She watches him as he walks to the front of the class and speaks to the model. Something good has come to her at last. She is overwhelmed and at the same time must maintain the African's attitude of self-composure, not scurry under her bench with fear. She will not show what it means to her. Already she is learning from him.

The next day at Renoir's, though, it is not so easy. It is first of all too early; the artist begins soon after dawn. He is in his garden-studio gazing at a bed of daffodils when she arrives. The patio has been transformed into his workspace, full of cabinets of materials and brushes, everything in order and ready for his attention. She has never been to the studio of an accomplished artist before. The maid leads her to a chair opposite him and he turns to her slowly. He is a thin man, the ravages of pain clearly marked on his face. Like everyone in Paris, Marie knows of his crippling arthritis and his refusal to surrender to it, but she did not expect to see it so clearly. A pair of crutches lies against a fence. There is also a readiness in him, though, his back ramrod straight, if only kept so by willpower.

He wears the white linen hat that is his trademark, his graying hair beneath. He is probably just over fifty though looks far older.

"We will begin with some questions, Mademoiselle, yes?"

She nods. His voice startles her. It is smooth, intelligent, much younger than the look of his body.

He stands and begins to walk around her, resting on the crutch to keep his balance. He studies her like he studied his daffodils, his small eyes that will not let her go. Near him is another one of his paintings of a nude, resting on a chair. It is clear that for Renoir, the skin is an envelope, a place to paint his beautiful colors, but says little of what might be inside, certainly not the pain that is inside of him.

"Tell me, for whom have you modeled?"

She mentions a few names, no one important. She is lucky she has not had to stand on the street corners of Montmartre looking for customers as so many do, a hair's breadth from selling her body.

"Do you object to taking off your clothes?"

"I prefer not to." She does not like to think what he would make of her covering of flesh, and besides, she is too thin. Her body tightens at the thought of it.

He touches her hair, plaiting it with his fingers. He is so close, she can smell his breath: the morning fish he ate, the coffee and croissant.

"Where are you from?"

"The countryside, near Plouigneau, in Normandy." She thinks of the seaside near her town, the boats on the gray ocean where they would go in the summer and the hot biscuits covered in butter she and her brothers ate. She will not let herself think of René.

"And how long have you been in Paris?"

"Three years." Her father stormed out of their house when she said she was leaving to be an artist, her mother no longer alive. Dying, the woman had slipped a velvet purse into her hand. Others were near, so it was only later that she unfolded it and found the money, enough to get her to Paris and keep her alive for a month or two. As she was leaving, René's sister met her at the carriage and spat in her face. But why should she stay, a dead man's wife? What was the purpose? When he was alive and they walked together in the fields, the glow inside of her felt better than any painting, but that left when she buried him. The decision to leave was easy.

He lets her hair go, returns to his chair, and picks up his cup of tea. He is the old painter again. His knuckles jut out from the crippling illness as he lifts the cup, but his brow smooths. He has made a decision. There is a cup near her, but she is too nervous to drink.

"Gleyre says you have ability. You know what I think of women painters?" He sets the cup back on the saucer, his hand trembling so that the cup almost falls. He ignores it and waits for her answer.

"No." She looks at him with neither challenge nor fear.

"Women are not biologically suited to a life in the arts any more than this bed of daffodils." He sweeps his frail arm toward the flowers. "It is illogical that the painter's subject should paint itself. Still, it does no harm, and when you are a mother you can impart what you have learned to your son."

He sounds like her father, like all the voices she must fight against. He says nothing for several moments, and she imagines she can hear bees walking on the petals of his daffodils.

"You will not need to take off your clothes. I will give you a costume. I am beginning a new canvas. I will talk to you about painting when I can. Please arrive on time."

"Thank you, Monsieur." Marie stands, her heart flapping. She will miss Gleyre's in the morning, but it does not matter. Other studios are open later. All she can see now is the larger room she will rent, and where she will put her easel. My God, his paintings go for thousands, and he will talk to her about art! It will not be hard to get a model with the money she will earn.

"And what do you think of my work Mademoiselle?" he asks as she is preparing to leave.

.He points to another canvas, of a Venus-figure beside a lake. This one looks stilted and foolish, as though he is trying to be a classical painter. Of course she will not say that. She wonders if being with him will make her father's child again, silent and unsure.

"I admire it a great deal, Monsieur." She keeps her face impassive. The pinks and lavenders of the model's flesh are deft, but the pose of the woman, like some kind of frozen goddess, seems ridiculous. It is as though Renoir is turning his back on his earlier work, and all that he and the others invented. And yet, with each passing year, his fame and the prices of his paintings only grow.

"You do not, I know that."

She looks at him with steady eyes and wonders at her ability to lie.

"And how do you know that?"

"It is obvious in how you glanced at it when you first walked in, how you glance at it now."

"You are wrong, Monsieur. I am only jealous."

"We shall see if you have reason to be jealous. Bring your drawings when you come next week. I will look at them."

He will look at her work! It is too much to have hoped. She is confused as to why she was not honest with Renoir, but does not want to think about that. Perhaps in knowing each other, they will both learn something. She certainly will—from his ability to live through all that poverty in his youth while making such great art, and now his dismissal of his pain, as though it does not exist.

Outside his apartments, the city is alive with morning traffic and the usual crowds. Young women in heavy skirts and tiny corseted waists scurry about their business; men in shiny hats and waistcoats walk firmly to assignations; children play. A noisy demonstration with placards and speeches gathers at the end of the boulevard.

Marie stares after the corseted women, their waists so small, it is hard to know how they can breathe. Her only corset is a ten-year-old thing that she uses when she must, though lately has been going without it. Recently she has seen one or two other women in Montmartre without them, as though women like her are creating the fashion of the future. She hopes they are. To breathe is what all women must do, breathe as easily as cows and sheep and all the men on earth. How can her gender achieve anything, if it must be continually tied up in string?

She starts across the street toward the Café de Nouvelle Athènes. Always when she passes it, she feels a chill. It is here that Renoir and the others came as young artists and drafted their revolutionary charter to remake the art world and invent Impressionism. Modeling for Renoir, she is now part of that, no matter how small. Today the Impressionists live in great chateaux off their proceeds. Just last month, Claude Monet sold a painting to a New York department store magnate for one million dollars!

"I am an artist," she says aloud. Everything that has happened has been worth it. "My family will see." She stands straighter and fills her lungs with air. She thinks of the paintings she will sell, even the great house she will live in. Yes, it is possible if she works hard. Rosa Bonheur lives in her own château. Why not have such dreams?

The shouts of the street demonstration become louder, but she ignores them. All of this has nothing to do with her. But then someone jostles her and steps on her skirts, and when she looks up, the demonstrators are quickly filling the intersection. It has something to do with the army, the name Dreyfus, voices shrieking, *"Vive l'armée"*. She tries to get away, but is quickly trapped in the sea of anger, bodies pushing her against a building until she can hardly breathe. A fight breaks out a few feet away, and the flash of a knife comes not an arm's length from her skirts.

Somehow she is able to turn down a side street, blood pounding in her ears, and catch her breath. She closes her eyes and wills herself to relax. : She breathes. She is an artist. She repeats it several times, though the blood still pounds in her ears.

III

"But this is *fantastic!* Marie." Abdul beams when she tells him, both of the modeling and the fact that Renoir will look at her drawings. A good word from such a famous painter, and she will be on the walls of a downtown gallery in no time. She does not speak about the demonstration. The sooner it is out of her mind the better.

"We must celebrate."

He is in the crowded anteroom with the others washing brushes and preparing for class. She never comes here if she can help it, but today she does not care. The job for Renoir and the demonstration have made her not want to be alone. Near Abdul she is safe. Next to him is a young man with frail skin and garnet-red hair, who looks at the ground as she draws near.

"Marie—you must to meet my new good friend Alexander Simon, the well-known photographer and artist, all the way from New York City. His father owns a great bank that shines down Fifth Avenue, from the top of the island to the bottom. New York City is an island, is it not?"

"Yes, it is an island, but my father does not own a great bank," the boy answers. "He is merely a manager."

"But it is on Fifth Avenue, yes? It is nearly the same thing! You must speak proudly of your parent, Alexander, particularly your father. Alexander, please to meet my new good friend and wonderful artist Marie Clouseau."

The young man looks at her. When she shakes his hand, she feels the softness of youth, but his hazel eyes are pinpointed with intelligence. As the African continues to talk, they look at each other and smile.

"I shall rent a carriage and we will drive to the country," Abdul continues, sweeping his cape over his shoulder. "We will toast Marie's good fortune with champagne and make paintings, and Alexander will take his photographs."

True to his promise, Abdul leaves Gleyre's halfway through the session, then reappears two hours later as Marie and Alexander are exiting onto the street. Her work was good this morning, she is sure it is because of Renoir. The sun is high and she is hungry. She had almost decided Abdul's picnic was a figment of his imagination when she sees him. He is on the seat of a small brougham above a sturdy white pony. He laughs and waves, then jumps down from the seat and flings open the doors, to reveal a basket brimming with roast chicken and other delicacies, along with two bottles of champagne.

Of course, he has managed this. He can manage anything, she decides. She wonders, not for the first time, who his family is and where he has come from, this magician from Africa, his pockets always bulging with flower petals and coin. The studio is rife with rumors—some say he is the son of a prince, others that his father owns a diamond mine or he is the son of an African ambassador.

Whenever she tries to ask, he laughs.

Three hours later, the two of them are resting in a field beneath a large poplar tree on the edge of a vineyard, the food long eaten, and Alexander rummaging in the seat of the carriage. Perhaps they are fifteen kilometers from the city, surrounded by countryside. Flies buzz lazily about them, butterflies. At the midpoint of the afternoon, no one, least of all insects, has the energy to move. Marie studies the wings of a bee, dozing on the leaf of a dandelion a few inches from her nose.

Abdul, lying on his back, turns to her. She has not been so near a man since René, perhaps a meter away. She puts the thought out of her mind.

"You are very lucky, Marie. I know this." As he speaks he rubs his chest with his hand, so large it could cover her face. Fantastic rings adorn his fingers, one of the face of a grinning wolf.

"My people would say that God shines on your heart."

She blushes. "I hope you are right. And who are your people?"

He grins and turns back to the sun. She will not let it go, though. She has seen so few Africans in Paris, not even twenty; she has no idea where he lives. "Why do you not tell me?"

His eyes are closed, only his profile facing her. "Because the past is of no consequence."

"But that is not true. We are composed of our past. It is our past that confronts our future. I am who I am today because of my past, and that is where I must plant my dreams."

He opens his eyes and looks at her. Even Marie is surprised by what she has said. In Abdul's presence, she can speak so clearly about what is true, and she is not afraid. An image of her father comes to her, his face red with pain on the day she left, and then her sister-in-law, so much anger in her eyes that Marie would dare live a life beyond widowhood. All she could do was scurry off into this future that even she did not believe in.

"You have heard stories, Marie, so I will now tell you the truth." He stands, wipes the grass off his hands, and sweeps open his cape. "Senegal is my mother. My father was a wealthy merchant."

He pauses and looks down at her for emphasis, a forced smile on his lips. "He was not a prince, nor did he own a diamond mine, but money was not foreign to our house." Another pause, another large sweep of the cape. "When I was twelve, he sent me to Algiers for my studies. When I was twenty, I came to Paris to begin my career. So you see, that is all there is to it! The secret is revealed!" He finishes and bows. For a moment a shadow passes over his face, but when Marie looks up, she sees only a flock of birds, flying across the sun.

He wraps his coat back around his shoulders. "Look at him. How excited he is!" Marie follows Abdul's gaze to Alexander at the carriage, carrying his equipment toward them. "We did not bring our paints, but Alexander goes nowhere without his camera. He told me he arrived two months ago, all by himself. His father is a friend of the Baron de Rothschild, did you know? He has stayed at his estate, but says little about the Baron or his father. All of my life I have wanted to look through such a device. It is the new world! Did you know, Marie, they can even make pictures that move?"

"Yes, I have heard."

"And if you could use such a device, what kind of art would you make?"

"The same as the art that I make today. I would tell the truth."

He smiles at her, his eyes soft. "Yes, I am sure you would."

He rushes to Alexander as he approaches with his equipment.

"Will it talk to us?"

"Cameras do not talk, Abdul." Setting up the equipment, the boy is much more confident than he was in the studio, a light veil of perspiration above his lip.

"Ah, but you are wrong. With the right eye, there is nothing they cannot say! You, Alexander, have the right eye!"

"How do you know? You have never seen my photographs."

"You do not have to look at the work of a true artist to know of their talent."

The boy smiles. In the full sun, his impossibly red hair is streaked with yellow, freckles prominent on his pale skin. Marie thinks of the boy's background, his father a New York banker, a friend of the Baron de Rothschild. She wonders if the boy and his father are Jews, like she has heard about the Baron. It is hard for her to imagine a person who is not of the church, and yet if she is honest, the religion of her birth is also part of her past now. When she thinks of it she can remember only the white lace her mother stitched so carefully for her first mass and how the sunlight poured down that day like syrup. Afterwards all the children ate buttercake and drank chocolate, and when she slept that night, she dreamt of angels.

Marie no longer goes to mass since coming to Paris. She thinks of the priest in her town and how displeased he was when she said she was leaving. Still, when the bells of a cathedral wake her in the morning, she lets the sound move through her body and cleanse her. What sounds or prayers cleanse the Jews, she wonders. She knows nothing of their rituals, but imagines them as secret and elaborate, thick with gold. The boy moves expertly to set up his tripod and attach the bulky camera. He disappears beneath a black cloth attached to the top of the camera box, then reemerges.

"Who wants to go first?"

"Is there film?" Marie asks.

"We do not put the film in yet. That is done after the picture is arranged."

"What picture shall we take?"

"Any that you like." The boy smiles in such a welcoming way; so what if he is a Jew? He will not bite her. Perhaps the priests have been wrong about this as well. For now, the camera is pointed toward the poplar tree, so that its leaves would fill the frame in an umbrella of green. "Marie?"

He motions to her, and she will not stand on ceremony.

"What you see will be inverted," the boy says. "That is from the mirror inside."

When she puts her head under the black veil, there is, for a moment, only darkness and then she sees it, the fantastic, upside-down image of the tree arching in its fullness to fill the frame, as another flock of birds moves in a slow *V* across the bottom of the picture, from one side to the other. With each beat of her heart, the picture changes, wondrous in its strangeness. Since the beginning, this is all that artists have wanted, to hold time in their hands like this and freeze it. She realizes that the impossible is now within their grasp. Monet and the rest saw exactly this on the coast of Normandy in the sixties when they were Alexander's age and she was not yet born. The very first photographers, not much older, worked by their side and together they changed art forever.

If time could be held like this, the impression, the artist's momentary glance, was all that mattered. Life as it is, not as it should be. The revolution was made.

IV

It is early evening when they leave, already thunder and lightning and a bad spring storm. If only they had left sooner, but Abdul insisted on taking as many photographs as possible, and now they are forced to drive the poor rented pony on a road that is more mud than gravel. Too soon it will be flooded, and if they cannot locate a detour, they will sleep in mud. If only there were somewhere to stop for the night—then she remembers a young woman who toured Gleyre's studio a few weeks before. Gleyre had asked Marie and a few others to share tea with the woman, and she had invited them to sketch at her estate in the Délices Forest. Perhaps if they take the newer road through the forest, they will find it. What she and her husband will think of the small company, Marie cannot imagine, but she is too wet to care. Abdul and Alexander agree they should try and in addition, the new road will be less flooded. Because they pretend to be chivalrous, both of them ride above steering the horse, making Marie shiver alone in the carriage. One window is broken and a second is missing. With every crack of lightning, the African laughs, or booms out a traveling song, in some guttural language of his ancestors. How tired her body is, bumping on every rut in the road and sliding on the seat wet with rain. But maybe God is shining on her because after just an hour on the new road, she catches sight of a sign for the Pousson estate lit by a small lamp and, a few moments later, can see the modest, two-story château before them, alive with welcoming light.

Soon enough they are at its door, and though the servant who opens it is taken aback by the motley group, the young woman quickly appears, and recognizes Marie in spite of her sopping hair.

"Please excuse me and my friends, Madame Pousson. Do you remember? We met at Monsieur Gleyre's studio?"

"But of course!"

Marie looks down at a small Pomeranian, barking so loudly with fear and excitement that she must raise her voice to be heard. With only a gas lamp in the entryway, there is not much to see of the country home beyond its stone walls and floor. Madame Pousson calmly motions to a servant, who carries the dog to another room.

"I had not meant to visit so soon, but we had a picnic at a nearby vineyard and got caught in the storm. And then I remembered that you live nearby and so we have found you."

"And I am so glad you did! Not only do you visit me, but you allow me to be of service to you. Come in, it is wet. We will stable your horse, and you will stay with us."

Gabrielle Pousson's brown saucer eyes open wide at the group, especially at Abdul who stands in one corner of the entryway, a dark, sodden figure towering above her. A small wrinkle of concern crosses her forehead, but otherwise she betrays no surprise, nor any displeasure at the water and mud they have brought into her home. She cups her fingers at her tiny waist, her chest moving in and out in steady breaths, a slight flush the only sign of emotion. With a smartness that Marie could not have managed, she instructs one of the servants to stable the pony, and another to show them rooms where they might wash and change into dry clothes. Marie can smell a beef stew somewhere in the house and other fine aromas that make her nearly faint with hunger. Madame Pousson grabs her hands and kisses them.

"Thank you for coming," she says in a voice that only Marie can hear. Marie thinks of the young woman at the studio, so shy and intimidated by the small group of art students that Marie had felt sorry for her. Here she is entirely at ease.

"Thank *you*, Madame."

"Gabrielle, please."

"Yes, Gabrielle. My friends are also artists, you know, and Alexander has a camera! In the morning, he will take a picture of you and your husband."

"He will?"

"Most assuredly. I will see to it myself."

Within the hour the three travelers are together again, before a fire in the Pousson sitting room, waiting to be called to dinner. The cook will prepare two extra capons. They will have a fine feast indeed. On a table near Marie is a book written in Russian and a pair of women's spectacles, laid on an open page. It makes her wonder about Gabrielle Pousson, the young woman who seemed so timid at Gleyre's, yet able to read Russian novels.

Marie picks it up and admires the foreign writing, but her eyes grow tired. It is just good to rest, she realizes, tired from the drive through the storm and the day of so much excitement, first with Renoir and then the demonstration. She thinks again of the artist and his crippling illness, still working to make art. Gleyre makes art in spite of anonymity, Renoir in spite of pain. Though her vision is so different, they both have already taught her.

"This is good luck indeed, Marie," Alexander whispers. "How do you know these people?"

"Madame Pousson came to Gleyre's a few weeks ago, I think to taste the bohemian life, so now it has followed her home."

Abdul, uncharacteristically silent, pulls a quilt more tightly around his shoulders and huddles near the fire. The light of the fire flickers in his face, creating shadows like the birds across the sun. He is a puzzle to Marie. There is a darkness in him, equal to his surprising smile, that she does not understand. Alexander pours them more wine, and she allows herself to be drawn into the drowsy silence of the fire, closing her eyes.

"Good evening," a sturdy voice sounds from across the room.

Marie opens her eyes to a well-dressed man of about her age striding toward them, Gabrielle on his arm. Her first impression of Gregoire Pousson is of grace and strength, as though he were an athlete. Blond with fine features, he could be her brother.

"I welcome you to my home!"

Alexander stands and offers his hand, his head nodding in polite salute as Gabrielle introduces them. Marie offers her hand.

Abdul, silent throughout, abruptly shoots up from his chair, the quilt dropping to the floor, and bows deeply.

"Abdul Farid Nadir Mbaye. My father is greatly honored by

your acceptance of his son in your home." His voice is loud and stiff and Marie realizes she has never heard his full name before.

"As my father is honored by your presence," says Gregoire. "Come. The food will be cold soon. It is time to eat."

Still drowsy from the fire, Marie wakens to the smell of the waiting dinner, and soon all five of them are eating in silence around a table thick with food—beef stew, capon with truffles, artichokes in mayonnaise. At last she looks up long enough to take a drink of wine. The three of them are a ragtag group—the young red-headed boy, the African, and herself—in dry, borrowed clothing that hardly fits. She wonders why the Poussons are so welcoming, different from other French she knows who at most would have given them shelter in a barn. But then the conversation begins and soon they are talking with animation about Alexander's camera, Abdul's wondrous travels—his eyes sparkling, his teeth flashing as he throws his head back in laughter—Marie's art, and she is only happy.

"You will model for Renoir and you speak of that with pride?" Gregoire's face is red, the muscles on his neck strained. The dinner is finished, coffee and pastry before them and Alexander's camera, unpacked and on a side table.

Gabrielle touches his arm. "Perhaps they do not know."

"They do not know? They do not read the papers? How could they not know?" He cracks open a paper by his plate, his voice strained: "This is what your Renoir has said about Dreyfus, the *Jew* he calls him. 'Of course he is guilty and I am finished with the Jews. It is a waste of money, all of these trials. There is no innocence where Jews are concerned.'"

"Who is Dreyfus?" Marie asks too quickly, and then a moment later remembers the afternoon demonstration, the shouts of *Vive l'armée* and the other demonstrators that shouted for Dreyfus. She looks down at the floor and speaks softly. "Oh yes, Captain Dreyfus, I remember."

Gregoire shakes his head in disgust as Gabrielle touches his arm. "You must excuse my husband. His firm is defending Captain Dreyfus and he is naturally full of emotion."

"It is not my employer who causes emotion but injustice." He rips into a piece of bread and points a finger at her, his fine, eagle features swooping down on her, making her want to flee. "From the very first there was never any evidence of treason, so it was manufactured. Now the government, embarrassed, has only been covering its tracks while the young captain has been rotting on Devil's Island for the last five years! Hordes are marching in the streets, Gabrielle, and your friends do not know."

Alexander looks up with interest. "You are defending him?"

"Yes. Not me, but my employer Edgar Demange. I have compiled important papers in his case. And there is absolutely no evidence, I tell you! He is only twenty-eight with a wife and children and his life is ruined. Everything was manufactured and the government launches trial upon trial to keep him imprisoned so they do not have to admit their mistake."

Candlelight flickers in the boy's eyes. "My father has given money for his defense."

"Really?" Gregoire does not hide his surprise. "That is excellent. And are your people Hebrews?"

Alexander touches the tablecloth. "Yes."

"That is fine. We have no prejudice in this household, do we Gabrielle?"

She shakes her head.

He turns to Marie. "I am sorry I have taken away your pleasure at your new position, but Auguste Renoir is not the simple appreciator of beauty, as his paintings would have you think. There is actually a rift among the artists over this case, did you know? Renoir, Degas, Cézanne on one side, the rest on the other. Monsieur Degas runs through the galleries screaming 'Kill the Jews.' Their famous compact against the Salon is long in the past. I am afraid your Impressionism is dead."

V

The silence in Renoir's garden is complete, a reduction of time and sunlight to this one moment, that has expanded to include everything in Marie's universe, only broken by the smallest sound of Renoir's brush touching his canvas or dipping into paint. She holds her head still in the pose so that she can see only a square of branch and leaf on the elm tree behind him; that is her world today, the bird that lights on the branch, the slight ruffle of a leaf. Peeking through the leaves are pockets of blue sky, and then miraculously, like some great roar, Marie hears the distant church bells of a late morning mass.

Renoir has dressed her in a colorful day dress and shawl, loosening her hair to rest on her shoulders, and put a bunch of daffodils in her arms. A painter must work outside, he instructs, to see the color of light and shadow. There is every color of the rainbow in shadow, can she see it?—then reaches out with his paint brush to point out squares of gray-lavender, gold, green, resting beneath a bush.

He has told her many things about art in the last week: that his hands ache in the morning from his arthritis, but painting is a wonderful remedy; that when one paints one must be 'stupid', to not use the mind and only the senses; that painting is joy; that it is art not nature that makes one want to be an artist, so Marie must spend as much time in museums as at her easel; that one must paint life as it is, not as the imagined perfection of the Greeks. This last point Marie knows comes from the Impressionists' rejection of the Salon's old-fashioned ideals—Greek myths meticulously staged in musty studios, political allegories—nothing of real life, and she agrees. As far as she can tell, though, his new paintings of women are equally idealized, not life as it is, but life as he wishes it to be.

About her own work, he has said little, only nodded his head and said that she will learn from him. Her heart beat so violently in her chest when she showed him her drawings that she thought she might faint. He must have seen the color drain from her cheeks, because he invited her for a cup of tea. After that it has become their ritual, a cup of tea before she leaves and he takes his lunch, each day at one, and now, today, the week is over, though not their work. The canvas is hardly begun.

He nods to show they are finished for the day, and after she has changed and returned to the garden, she sees there is money under her teacup, enough to buy the linen she will need for painting, a full bag of groceries, and even a few francs more. His talk of museums has also inspired her, so today will be a true celebration—at least two galleries at the Louvre and afterwards the market.

Of course she has not spoken to him of Dreyfus, any of that. What would be the point? He is her employer and she will work for him as long as she can because he gives her good money, twice as much as what she gets from others, and because of who he is and what he can do for her. Gregoire Pousson is no doubt right, but he has never had to model for food, nor build a career as an artist. Renoir's bigotry is a taste in her mouth she will have to swallow. In fact, it has become difficult for her to imagine, such thoughts coming from this man, who confronts his disease with such courage. She will protect Alexander from him; of course they will never meet. Of all of them, Alexander was the most understanding. In the carriage on the way back from the Poussons, he brought it up, taking her hands in his. "You will work for Renoir," he said. "It is too great an opportunity. Please, you will not offend me. You are my friend, not his."

Now on the street outside Renoir's, her plan is to go directly to the galleries, but she cannot help herself. Now that she has money, the vegetables and fruit of Les Halles call too loudly. The market has been running continuously since the twelfth century. It is named the Belly of Paris, and there is no better term. Everything is here: cheeses of all variety, sea creatures from the Mediterranean, rabbits, huge sides of beef. She nearly runs there from his apartments, then wanders the stalls lazily, stroking the vegetables and ripe fruit. For a long time she is too inspired by the money in her skirt to care about anything but the meal she will make for herself and her new friends. She must have carrots, mushrooms from the countryside, a piece of lamb, as the dinner she will make grows in her mind. There is a wood range in her landlady's apartments, shipped all the way from America, with three burners and an actual oven. If she offers her some, she knows the woman will not object. Then, just as she is scolding herself for spending so much, she hears her name called near a flower stand and when she turns, sees the excited face of Gabrielle Pousson, rushing toward her.

"How good to find you, Marie."

Gabrielle pecks her on her cheek, her breath warm. "I went to Gleyre's and did not find you. I'd given up all hope, and here you are!"

The young woman's eyes must be permanently crinkled in a smile, Marie decides, Gabrielle's cheeks downy in the sunlight. Before Marie knows what has happened, the young woman has forcibly grabbed her arm and led her back into the center of the market, to buy her truffles and other delicacies Marie could never afford.

"I want champagne for lunch, don't you? You will be my guest. There is a tiny bistro where the frogs' legs are so good. It is always crowded, but I know we shall get a table."

When they enter, the bistro is full to capacity, but there is somehow space for them, and in minutes they are seated. Marie is enveloped in the warmth of the restaurant's aromas, the linen tabletops, and her new young friend beside her, turning and twisting in her chair to order just the right champagne and meal. When the waiter pours the champagne, Gabrielle drinks it quickly, her nose wrinkling in pleasure, sets her glass down, and pours more.

"Drink, drink," she coaxes Marie. "Garçon!" she calls out too loudly, to a young man a few feet away polishing glasses. "Bring us oysters while we wait. We must have food!" She clutches Marie's arm. "Oh, I love being alive. Don't you love being alive?"

Marie smiles.

"I love my husband, I love Paris, I love my new friend. May I call you my new friend?"

"Of course."

She kisses Marie's hand and laughs in a high-pitched voice, then lets her head fall to the table and buries it in her arms. Light shines on her sable hair, so brightly that it blinds Marie. "Shall I have a third glass? I know I like champagne too much. That is what Gregoire says. Soon we shall have to order another bottle." When she sits up her head is jerky, looking from one end of the restaurant to the other. Her thick hair falls too quickly across her forehead. She is no longer the calm young woman of a week ago, but someone else, a nervous racehorse perhaps, a hummingbird.

"Is everything all right, Gabrielle?"

"Of course it is all right."

She laughs as the waiter sets down a plate of oysters. All are open save one, tucked to the side. She works at prying it open, her mouth grimacing, but her knife slips and she cuts her finger.

"Ohh!"

"Be careful, Gabrielle."

"I am fine." She absently sucks at it, then holds it against a napkin. "Have you heard the news?"

"What news?"

"About the writer, Émile Zola?"

Marie shakes her head. "No."

"You haven't? Then I will tell you." She picks up the knife again and works at another oyster. "He published a very long letter to the president in support of Captain Dreyfus and against the government. The state has arrested him for libel. Gregoire left three nights ago to prepare his case with Demange, and I have not seen him since."

As she speaks, the happy crinkles around her eyes disappear, her voice on the verge of tears. "He says they should arrest him for libel as well. During the day he works for Demange—they are launching Zola's defense with another lawyer—and at night he goes to the demonstrations. I am so worried!"

With the mention of the demonstrations, the shouts of the last three nights, the torches and footfalls through the streets, come to Marie. "Best to stay inside tonight," her landlady had said when they passed on the staircase. The first night there were crowds in the street screaming "Death to Jews!" and the sound of broken glass. Marie closed her window and took out her rosary.

There are suddenly tears in Gabrielle's eyes, her small body restraining sobs.

"I am so glad I found you. I was hoping I would find you. I have no one else to talk to. My mother and father are Royalists and his parents are dead."

There is nothing for Marie to say. She looks at her with sympathy.

"I don't understand why he acts this way. Our wedding was so beautiful, and my dress, he said I looked like a bed of roses, the most beautiful thing he'd ever seen. Of course I am proud of him. I am so proud of him."

"Yes."

"What shall I do?"

Marie says nothing.

"They say it will pass," Gabrielle says. "That the anger against the Jews always happens and then it passes."

"I'm sure that's true." Marie has heard this too.

"You know, sometimes I have these terrible thoughts that Dreyfus has stirred it all up and now Zola. What right has he? Such a great writer?" Gabrielle turns to her, a frightened expression on her face. "I am so sorry my husband talked to you the way he did. You aren't angry at us, are you?"

"Of course not." Marie knows Gregoire is right.

"You are so lucky."

"Why am I lucky?" When Marie thinks of her life in her small room—her poverty, her loneliness—there seems little to be grateful for.

"Because you have a purpose, like Gregoire. Perhaps that is what upsets me the most, the days in the country alone with the servants, and so much is happening. On and on, my life marches, and I thought it would be so grand. My mother says that when I have children, I will be happy. What do you think?"

"I am sure you will." Marie's own lack of children is not a sorrow for her, but she assumes she is different.

"Yes, perhaps." Gabrielle does not sound convinced. "But promise me, you will make me part of your art one day, if you can?"

"Of course." The thought of painting Gabrielle occurs to her for the first time. She wonders if Gregoire would allow it. She imagines her unclothed at her bath, her pale skin and rich brown hair. She would put a vase of white tulips beside her, the dog asleep near his mistress.

Marie takes her hand. "You must not worry, Gabrielle. Gregoire is a courageous man, and he is doing what he knows to be right. Everything will come out well in the end. I am sure of it." Marie can hear herself speak the platitudes women have told each other for centuries, but she doesn't know what else to say.

"I suppose you are right." Gabrielle is unconvinced, but their meal arrives, a reason for both to pour more champagne and divert themselves with food.

By the time they are on the street, the young woman is nearly her old self, so long as Marie promises to visit her.

Marie has enjoyed the lunch, but this day must belong to her. Soon enough she will have to return to Renoir. She can only think of building her canvas, buying paint, walking the galleries of museums. It is not easy to get free of Gabrielle, though. First, she wants to return to the market, then take Marie to her favorite milliner. The basket of food on Marie's arm is already growing ripe and she must take it back to her rooms. There is a carriage to be found for Gabrielle, though, goodbyes to be made. Marie asks if she may make charcoals of her in a week or two, she does not mention the real work that she has in mind, and Gabrielle is overcome with joy.

VI

As the carriage drives away, Marie sighs with pleasure at the day ahead, her stomach nicely full and mind lulled by champagne. She walks briskly toward her rooms—first she will deposit the food in her landlady's cool cellar, then go out again to buy painting linen and paint. She would sing, if she could, she is that happy, but then, rounding a corner, the refuse of the last three nights of demonstrations confronts her: dirty banners that hobble her ankles, filthy phrases scrawled on buildings—Death to the Jews, *Mort aux juifs!* and the others screaming *Vive l'armée!* She thinks of Alexander, his tender face and serious expression when he made his photographs in the country, and she must restrain herself from being sick. Why must any Jew die, least of all Alexander? How is he connected to Dreyfus, Zola, any of this?

It is only the feel of the painting linen under her fingers that soothes her. After depositing her basket in the cellar, she has rushed to her favorite supplier's and now greedily strokes several bolts of fabric, searching for the one that is exactly right. The feel of the linen, even its scent, must speak to her. She has not forgotten

Dreyfus; in fact, she has made the decision to attend Zola's trial. According to Gabrielle, it will start in a few days' time. Today, though, belongs to her. God how she wants to begin the painting; it will be like diving into a fresh pool of water, after being parched for days, all the difficulty of her own life and now this Dreyfus business healed. There was a pond on her father's farm where she and her brothers would swim each summer. She can still feel that—the heat of the sun on her skin and then the quick splash of the water, so cold at first, until she dove under, and then it was like swimming in silk.

Painting is the same for Marie; there is hardly a difference, wrapping herself in the color, the smells, the hour upon hour that she can lose herself. She will prepare carefully for this painting, meticulously. (Has she already learned that much from Renoir, his slow ritual of lining up his many paint brushes, each ready for a different task as though he were a surgeon?) After she builds the frame for the canvas, she will nail the linen across each edge, working to make sure that all sides of the material are equally stretched. Then she must wet the fabric to let it shrink to its new surroundings, but that is just the beginning. When it dries, it will have to be sized with the proper mixture, to reduce absorbency and create a ground. There is no better method for this than brushing the material with rabbit-skin glue, made literally from the hides of rabbits, a technique used since the Renaissance.

It is late afternoon when she returns home, her arms full. She is hungry, but there is no time to make the meal she planned earlier. There is never time. All domestic chores must come second to her art. She eats something quickly, then begins. Since the glue needs to be heated overnight, its preparation is the first task, the small flecks of rabbit hide mixed with water, then warmed in her hearth. When it is ready in the morning, it will have the consistency of jelly.

She carefully measures the flecks into a pot, adds the correct amount of water, and sets it on a smoldering log. It must be brought to boiling but no more, as the glue would lose its adhesion, so she must watch it carefully. As it heats, it lets off a slight animal scent that reminds her of the countryside, and her thoughts drift there as she works, building the frame from the wood slats she stores under her bed. It will be evening soon, a cool breeze coming in through her open window, the streetlamps softly glowing as night descends. 'Magic time', René called this time of evening. He took her to a village dance once, and they swirled and swirled until they fell into a bed of jasmine. He led her to a field behind her father's house where they lay together and in the morning he asked her father for her hand. They married in spring and by summer he was dead from influenza. The night before he died, he told her to go to Paris. René was not like other men. He said to live for both of them. Thinking of him puts so much longing in her heart. She told one of her cousins that their marriage was the best time of her life, and today she can barely see his face.

On the day of his funeral, she closed the door of her father's house and said, *I cannot face this,* then left a few weeks later for Paris. It happened and she came here to pursue her life.

She stands and checks the glue to make sure it has not gotten too hot—just before it reaches a boil she must take it off the log—which is when she hears the shouts, distant but growing quickly, so that by the time she has gone to her window, she can see the horde rounding the corner, fists raised, banners, a gash of hatred across each face, so violent they look like a herd of beasts. *Mort aux juifs! Mort aux juifs! Mort aux juifs! Mort aux juifs!* they scream. She can't keep from screaming herself. She holds both hands over her ears and slides to the floor.

VII

Marie's head pounds with a headache. She has taken a headache powder, but as she heads for the Palace of Justice and Zola's trial, she does not know how many hours she can stand it. The air is gray and cold beside the Seine, occasional stay dogs walking past. Why are there so many stray dogs in Paris, Marie wonders, ribs jutting out, fighting over scraps of food?

Her headache started an hour ago over coffee in their usual café, Alexander telling her and Abdul that he had purchased a ticket for America. His voice was matter of fact, but the reason for the return was obvious. His parents were worried by the riots in the streets, the chaos, the hatred against the Jews, that was published daily in American papers. In addition, a position had opened for him at the bank.

"But what about your camera?" Abdul had asked. He looked frightened to Marie, if he could have fear, the cords in his neck standing out tense and exaggerated. There was also a darkness under his eyes, as though he had not slept for days, his colorful coat smudged with dirt. That was when the pain behind her eyes began and she asked the bar boy for a headache powder.

"Do not fear, Abdul. My camera will travel with me on the ocean liner. Besides, there are good subjects in America as well. The best is a young woman I know, and if I am very lucky, I will be the first to take her engagement photo." When he said this, he blushed, and Marie realized he was speaking of his fiancée, though he had not said it in so many words.

That was an hour ago. Now as the three approach the Palace of Justice for the first day of Zola's trial, they are met by a striking scene. The front door to the Assizes Court is blocked by a crush of over two hundred barristers and reporters, bystanders climbing on the stone lions of the building and hollering against Dreyfus and the Jews. When the army tries to clear them away, young lawyers break into fights with the soldiers and the crowd cheers.

Marie should be at Renoir's, but she is here instead, and is glad. For the last week in the artist's studio, each day has followed the next in perfect daffodil silence, immune to the shouts of the night before. His gaunt straw face has said nothing, though he has put the newspaper with Zola's letter beneath his paints to scrabble on. Marie knows it is right that such a famous French writer has accused the government of this deceit, but she is a mouse where Renoir is concerned. Yesterday, posing for him, she was glad, for once, of the requirement to keep her head frozen, so she did not have to look at the newspaper's three-inch headline, *J'accuse…! Lettre au président de la République par Émile Zola*, screaming at her to speak, and she didn't.

Today her absence will speak. The crowds are so thick, though, they must enter through a side door, and once inside, there is only room to stand at a rear wall. When they are finally installed, Marie looks up at a magnificent ceiling painted with serpents and oak trees, the spear of Bacchus, a sepulcher—all haughty symbols to truth and justice. Tapestries line the walls. Far, far in the distance are the judges, tiny figures in black robes. Gregoire sits at a table near them, with two other men, also in robes; Gabrielle is somewhere near them. Zola, a gray, bespectacled man, is elevated in the defendant's box. He is president of the French Society of Authors whose works are translated into nearly every language on earth; he is the most famous writer in all of France, and he is on trial, for speaking the truth.

When the room finally quiets, the proceedings begin, but it is interminable. Time moves as though through syrup. Marie's head hurts less, but the powder has made her drowsy. Because they stand so closely, she closes her eyes and balances herself between her two friends, as the witnesses drone on. An army captain, a general, a war minister, other soldiers—each refusing to discuss evidence against Dreyfus because to do so would threaten state security. The defense had planned to defend Zola by proving the evidence against him was manufactured, but since the witnesses won't testify, that is impossible. The public in the top gallery cheers or shouts with each perceived victory or loss. By afternoon, a mob of over ten thousand has amassed around the courthouse, shouting its regular chant to kill all traitors and Jews, and a passerby is thrown into the Seine.

When it is finally over, it takes Marie and the others an hour to walk across the bridge to the Left Bank, but she can breathe now, outside of the courthouse. She has also done something useful, appeared in support of Zola. There is Marie, Alexander, Gregoire and Gabrielle; also Herzl, a young Viennese journalist who is covering the trial and has attached himself to Gregoire. Abdul has left them, Marie does not know why. He often leaves now, then returns at some unknown time. She has begun to worry about him, though no longer asks.

"I witnessed Dreyfus' degradation," the journalist is saying, when they are seated at a small outdoor café. His black eyes look at them with such accusation that it makes Marie feel guilty anew. "It was when they first stripped him of his medals and broke his sword," he says with a malicious grin.

"You must understand this person, Captain Dreyfus." Herzl

turns on Marie and Alexander, as though accusing them alone. "He is like a hero from some Dumas novel, so clean-shaven and handsome. To tell you the truth, I think he is slightly horrified by the anarchy of Gregoire and Demange. He is nearly a royalist!"

He pushes back the black curls that hang on his forehead, his skin dotted with sweat. "The first trial was secret. The night of the verdict, they led him into a courtyard. I was one of a few reporters. He was paraded in front of his officers like some donkey." He spits the word out with venom as his voice rises. "A colonel ripped his service ribbons from his uniform, then dragged his sword from its sheath and broke it into pieces. When they finished, they led him outside to a crowd of thousands that spat at him and threw dog excrement in his face.

"He stood with such proud posture through it all, and at that very moment a thought occurred to me that I cannot get out of my mind." He pauses and regards the entire table. "That assimilation for the Jewish people is nonsense, and that nothing will change for us until we have our own state!"

Herzl pounds the table with such force that Marie's glass trembles, then looks away from her and begins questioning Gregoire with intensity on some minutiae of the trial.

Marie lets out a breath. Thank God he has stopped looking at her. The shadow of the headache is still with her, and on top of that her exhaustion from the trial and the man's dreadful story. The evening before, the riots kept her up half the night, and tomorrow she must see Renoir again. On the edge of the Seine, the café catches the coolest breeze that blows jasmine on them from a nearby bush. There is the world, and then there are the problems of the world, Marie thinks. Why can't she simply live in the world, paint, enjoy people? A black dog wanders by, looking for scraps; a young woman in a red satin dress leads a young man who follows behind laughing. It is quieter now with the mob gone, and the young man's laughter echoes off the water. Gabrielle is sitting next to her, and has said little all evening.

"How are you?" Marie whispers, taking her hand, and Gabrielle looks up at her gratefully.

"Better, thank you." She speaks so softly that Marie must strain to hear. "I am with child," she says.

"You are?"

Gabrielle nods.

A happiness mixed with jealousy forms in Marie's chest that she does not understand. "Why that is wonderful! I am so glad for both of you."

"Yes." Gabrielle smiles. She looks truly happy.

"Alexander, did you hear?" Because Gabrielle has said it in the open, it is not a secret. Besides, Marie cannot stop herself.

"No? What?" He has been talking with Gregoire and the reporter, composed as he always is, asking questions with interest.

"Gabrielle and Gregoire are having a child!"

His face cracks into a broad grin. "Mazel tov! That is such good news. Congratulations!" Alexander stands and raises his glass as the others follow. Gabrielle blushes, moving up against Gregoire.

Alexander looks across at the reporter. "Do you remember our saying, Theodor? *Mit yedn kind, heybt zikh on di velt oyf's nay*...With each child, the world begins anew!"

It is very late, but Marie has found a second wind. Perhaps it is the news of Gabrielle's baby that has reinvigorated her, the new world Alexander promised and the good meal they all shared. She and Alexander have walked halfway across Paris and back, talking of every imaginable subject: what he will do when he returns—he will take the RMS Etruria, leaving from Liverpool in a fortnight; her plans for her painting; Dreyfus; the trial; art. When they left, Gabrielle and Gregoire were walking arm in arm. She cannot remember her more glowing. Gabrielle will make such a wonderful subject, even better now that she is pregnant. It is agreed that Marie shall come to their estate soon and begin the charcoal studies. Neither she nor Gregoire mind that it will be a nude. Perhaps Marie will need to cancel again with Renoir, but she does not care. She is finished worrying about a man who could hold such prejudiced views, and she will tell him so tomorrow.

She and Alexander stand on the Pont Royal, a bridge downstream from the Pont Neuf and nearly as old. The mob, thank

God, is long gone and asleep in their beds.

Further downstream is the Eiffel Tower, the fantastic metal edifice that is less than a decade old. Beneath it, obscured by trees and lit by only a crescent moon, is the large plot of land that will house the 1900 World's Fair in a year and a half, already under construction.

"Look Alexander," she says pointing to the plot. She likes Paris best with a crescent moon. There are more stars, like the nights in Normandy when she was a girl. A few twinkle over the top of the tower in a necklace. "I heard the other day, that, for the World's Fair, an electric sidewalk will carry visitors from one exhibition to the other. Can you imagine, traveling like that instead of walking? There will be a Palace of Electricity with all of Mr. Edison's inventions, and at night, the tower will be illuminated by 5,000 incandescent bulbs!" She turns to him. His red hair this late at night looks black. "You must come to see it, and with your wife too if you are married!"

Marie pictures them in her imagination, fine and beautiful, riding a handsome motorcar. Perhaps she will have more money then, and they will come to her large, bright studio for tea, with all of her paintings on the wall.

"Oh, you must, you must! Say you will."

He smiles. "Of course. Except if my wife is also with child," he adds shyly. He rests his elbows on the edge of the bridge and looks toward the tower. When it was first built, some people criticized it as a hideous monstrosity, but Marie liked it from the first.

"What is she like?"

He doesn't answer for a moment, just staring at the tower, and when he does, he shrugs. "I don't know. Beautiful. Very sweet. We have known each other since childhood. I'm not very good at describing people; that is why I'm a photographer. Imagine the difficulty I will have describing you and Abdul to her! Luckily I have your pictures."

Marie smiles. Against the stone of the bridge, she can feel the dampness of the morning that is coming.

"Someone at Gleyre's said they will show movies that talk. But I don't believe that. Do you think the twentieth century will be very different?"

"My father thinks so. Mr. Edison, he said, will remake the world. There will be devices from his electricity that we cannot now even imagine. Though he also says that many things, particularly people, will remain as they have always been, and we must be prepared for that as well."

A street cleaner passes silently behind them sweeping away the day's refuse. He is African, his face scarred like Abdul's, his eyes invisible in folds of wrinkles.

"Where do you think Abdul goes, when he is not with us?"

"I do not know."

She misses his laughing face and bright coat, that has become so dull with wear. She would like to wash it for him as he warmed himself in front of her fire, cook the meal she has waiting in her landlady's cellar. She would even pose for him if he asked. She thinks of his cobalt skin and scars. She wonders what it would be like to touch them and thinks of them under the linden blossoms when he walked like a king.

VIII

My God the woman's jewel is bright!

That is the first thing Marie thinks as she steps onto Renoir's patio. It is a deep red ruby color set in yellow brass that glitters at her so fiercely, it is all she can see. Then she sees its owner, a large-bosomed woman of thirty-five or six, with luxurious black hair and a still-attractive form, in heated debate with the painter, the two drinking coffee, laughing, eating pastries, as the visitor appraises his canvases spread out on numerous chairs.

"It's all brushwork with you, Auguste." The woman lifts her coffee cup firmly to her mouth and downs the rest of the drink. She has a bright glamour about her that makes it hard for Marie to turn away, her features chiseled and ideal. She could be an actress though she does not speak like one. "Where is your old innovation? The compositions could be Ingres or David, hanging in the Salon. It is only the subject matter that holds our interest."

Other than Marie's painting—Renoir has depicted her as a starry-eyed country girl with an armload of daffodils—the rest are nudes of the kind Marie particularly dislikes, stilted figures of idealized flesh, as though he is trying to paint Greek goddesses. Neither notice Marie, who hangs about on the edge of their conversation waiting to be spoken to or given a request. Why must she always wait, as though she has no thought of her own? Her chest is full with her mission today, and she is no longer afraid to look at the *J'accuse* of Zola's letter, yellowed and frayed beneath Renoir's brushes. Having not slept at all the night before, she will withstand her morning with him, perhaps he will even fire her when she makes her statement, and then she will sleep.

"And you are no longer so beautiful to look at yourself, Suzanne." Renoir smiles. "Which makes your meaningless critique particularly irrelevant."

She laughs. "Yes, but you still invite me and always will, because you know I am right. My advice is that you stop invalidating the revolution you helped to create. You are a great painter, Auguste, your painting of the *moulin* is one of the greatest paintings of the century. But the world moves on. You know they are now talking of Post-Impressionism?"

"Huh!" he grunts.

"Well, it is true, whatever you think, and it would do you good to go to some of the newer galleries. Look at the Dutchman Van Gogh, who is teaching us all over again how to paint. It is only a pity that he is dead." On the table is a small piece of pastry. She downs it quickly between her red lips and turns to Marie, pulling a card from her dress and handing it to her. So, the woman has been aware of her all along. When the older woman turns her gaze on her, something inside Marie lights.

"Visit me," she says. "I will pay you more than he does, and the conversation will be much more interesting."

"Mademoiselle Valadon, meet my new liege, Mademoiselle Clouseau. Marie, Suzanne Valadon, a true legend of Montmartre." Hearing the name, Marie's attention is riveted. So, this is the woman who began as the illegitimate daughter of a Parisian laundress. Valadon was Degas' model and lover, so talented that she, a self-taught artist, now hangs in the Luxembourg, alongside Degas and the rest of them. But that is not the only reason for her fame. Unconcerned with the thoughts of society, she refuses to divulge the father of her fifteen-year-old son though there are enough men still in love with her to make her a wife if she would let them.

Valadon swirls her skirts to face Marie head-on, the ruby brooch glistening on one breast, and grins at her warmly.

"I congratulate you on withstanding Monsieur Renoir. He is a great teacher, though. And kind when he gets around to it."

Valadon turns her smile back to the painter, kisses his cheek, opens her parasol, and leaves.

With her exit, the patio is invaded by emptiness. A maid in a starched white apron walks out to clear the plates of pastry crumbs onto a large tray, then retreats into the coolness of the house. Somewhere there are children's footfalls and laughter. Renoir nods at Marie and she takes her usual place. There is a fresh bouquet of daffodils to hold in her lap. The bees buzz in the background, she smells the ever-present linden blossoms now alive throughout the city and can hear his brush lightly scratching the canvas.

"So, what did you think of Valadon?" he asks.

He usually does not speak when he paints except to say something about art when it occurs to him. Her heart beats, and she despises herself for her lack of courage. Even that one question, and she finds it impossible to answer. Zola's headline *J'accuse* stares at her and will not let her go.

"I admire her." Her voice is barely audible.

"What was that?" Renoir makes a brushstroke, then tilts his head to appraise it.

"I think she is a great painter, and in addition she has lived with much courage." It is as though her heart is in her mouth when she speaks and she cannot see the trees and flowers around her for her fear.

Renoir is painting again. "Yes, I suppose, though women are not really meant to paint. A woman's place is as the subject of a painting, as you are of mine. Women are a symbol of beauty. How can a symbol paint itself?"

There is still the wave of fear, but she gets the words out anyway. "I do not agree with that." She has no idea how she sounds, soft or loud. It is enough that she has spoken.

Renoir is unperturbed, mixing his colors on his palette, appraising them, daubing them onto his canvas. "Yes, I am sure you don't agree. You have, afterall, come to Paris to be a painter, have you not? And how are you progressing in your career, Marie?"

She can feel tears forming in her eyes. Of course she is a failure. She has achieved nothing and except for jobs like this one, she barely has money to eat. "I am making my way."

"Of course you are."

The subject is closed. The painter studies a side of the canvas carefully and begins applying paint with a small brush. The daffodils in Marie's arms feel uncomfortable and sticky, and her tears are ready to fall, but she will not allow them. He will grin and say she may excuse herself, one more reason why her gender is unsuited to a life in the arts.

Zola's paper on Renoir's table seems to curl and brown, dying before her eyes, as he scrabbles a color onto the headline to test it before putting it on the canvas.

"What do you think of Zola?" Her voice comes out louder than she expected.

Renoir says nothing, but he grimaces and shakes his head. Minutes go by. A white dove alights on the vine-covered fence. The maid returns with a fresh pot of tea, ready for when they finish. It is clear he will not answer, so she speaks for him.

"I was not sick yesterday, you know. I went to Zola's trial. I am friends with one of his lawyers." She has said it, the worst that can be said, and all at once her fear disappears. In its place is something like an ocean wave that she can feel beneath her and draw strength from. It is like the waves of her childhood that she swam in on the coast of Normandy. Most girls do not swim, it is true, but her brothers took her once and showed her how, and it was easy from the start, so that every summer she would beg them to take her until they did. Why did someone not tell her this was the same, that being brave was merely a matter of finding the current that would send you so high, and then rest there beneath you, to carry you to your destination?

He puts his brush down and takes a drink of tea. "So, you are another one that has left me for Dreyfus," he says. "There have been so many." He does not seem so much angry as tired, even amused. "Even Valadon is with Dreyfus. Though she still deigns to visit me."

"Monsieur Dreyfus is innocent," Marie says forcefully. "It is only because he is a Jew that they accused him." She clutches the stems of her daffodils tightly, her fingernails digging into them. "And now Zola accuses all of us back, as he should, and I, for one, will support both as hard as I can." There is no separation now, between Marie's life and art. In fact, it is easy to say what is true, and she will do so now and into her future, happily and without regret.

Renoir's face contorts, reddening to his forehead. "Pah! The Jews," he spits forcefully into the bed of daffodils near his feet. "I am through with them!"

He stands, shaken, goes to a cupboard to retrieve a brush, spills the jar, bends with difficulty to take one, then returns to the easel.

"You know, Mademoiselle Clouseau, you are neither as talented nor as beautiful as Suzanne Valadon to engage in such conversation. It is not becoming." He sits back in front of the painting and works to compose himself.

"I say only what is true." For the first time that she has been with him, Marie can see beyond his patio wall, covered with its small white flowers, to the sunny day that will be there when she leaves, as though the gold of the daffodils has spread out over the city, and at the same time taken root in her heart.

"Did you know, the reason I chose you as a model?" He is now fully in his painting again, mixing colors, appraising, examining her pose intently. "Because you are a mouse, which you shall always be. Mouse With Daffodils, *Souris avec les jonquilles.* That shall be the title of our painting." He finishes something and puts down his brush. "Shall we have our tea? A bit early today, but Valadon has tired me." He stands and reaches out his hand to lead her to the table. If he was angry before, the feeling has left him. "Come, it is only the Jews that separate us. Let us kiss and make up."

Marie also is no longer angry, but is done with him and sees only the gold of the city that she wants to enter.

"No, Monsieur, not today, nor any day." She sets the flowers down on her chair and goes to the changing room. Her hands tremble as she unbuttons the costume, but that is of no consequence. All the churches in the city peal the hour, a great cacophony of the sound that is in her heart. When she returns to the patio and unfolds her parasol, she barely looks at him as she opens his gate and steps onto the street.

IX

There are moments in life, unbidden, when a sight comes, offering the ability to look backwards and forwards at once, and Marie enters that now.

It is as though time has stopped. She gazes about her, at women in swirling, pastel skirts, men in carriages, and at the same time, she is crawling through a field of daisies, her earliest memory, laughing and falling into flowers. Her red shoe steps onto the pavement, a dog barks, she laughs in the flowers and gazes at the sun. She gazes at the sun in Montmartre, and begins walking into the morning.

She will model for Valadon, but she will also be proud to stand on the street corners for artists to hire her, as Valadon herself used to do. She might also learn a trade until she can sell her paintings. A milliner, for example. Why has the thought never occurred to her? The only thing missing is Abdul to brag to about what she has done. So, she notices nothing wrong when she sees him in front of her rooms, there at the end of the day when she has finally had her fill of walking the galleries of the Louvre until dark: the Italians, my God! She stumbled upon the Italian wing by accident and could not leave, staring at a painting of the coronation of the Virgin, for an hour at least—the gold leaf of the young Mary's ascension outlined in the finest blues and pinks, notes of color so perfectly harmonized, she could nearly hear them. Then, on her way out, she was transfixed by Fra Filippo Lippi's *Old Man and Boy*. A simple portrait, the small boy looking into the face he will have decades in his future, the old man gazing down at his past; behind them both, a path winding through the mountains of their combined lives.

Why do paintings bring her to tears, she wonders, such beauty and truth combined? She almost runs to Abdul, she is that happy.

Only a gas lamp illuminates his face in the moonless night and it is not yet late enough for more than a few stars.

He leans against the balustrade, a dark figure in a navy sweater and trousers. It takes a moment for her to realize she has never seen him without his coat of many colors or rings. Were it not for his African face, he could be any French laborer in the stockyards. Except for his ceremonial scars, his brow is clear, his posture erect. A traveling bag hangs on his shoulder.

She is out of breath from rushing to him, ready to speak, and then something like the wing of a night moth touches her cheek and stops her. Maybe the hesitance comes to her from his expression, smooth and decisive. He touches her arm. Looking back, it is this one moment she wishes she could have made longer, the moment before the finding out. She wishes she could have filled that moment with every painting in the Louvre, everything that is beautiful on earth, but still it would not have been enough.

"Marie, Alexander. He is dead." He looks at her steadily.

"What?"

She will not allow the words in. Just this morning they shared coffee, his hair red and alive in the early dawn, his hazel eyes sparkling. They held hands, and she could feel his heartbeat; she can feel it now.

"Where is your coat?" She tries to catch his eyes and make him grin his bright grin, but he will not do it.

"They killed him, Marie." Without the coat, he is thinner, even cold in the spring evening. A stray dog runs by, its ribs visible. She sees Alexander's eyes and his long red eyelashes. They kissed when they parted, his soft cheek touching hers, still a boy's with hardly a beard.

"He was taking pictures of a synagogue. Three men were praying. A pack of them came in, broke windows, smashed his camera, beat them."

In spite of herself, Marie pictures the scene, yellow stained glass crashing to the floor, rays of sunlight broken into jagged pieces, pain. Alexander took her to a synagogue just the week before. Because she is a woman, they had to walk to the balcony, but they were closer to the golden glass there. It was not so different from a cathedral—less grand, perhaps, and not so austere, with more sunlight. Jews did not believe in hell, Alexander said. Maybe that was why.

"Then they hung them, all four, from the ceiling."

Now the crashing starts and with that the tears though she hardly feels them. It takes her to the place of René, the feeling she hoped never to feel again, the terrible smell death makes in her mind. She sees Alexander's dear face and wishes she could cradle him. There is the on of a person's life and then the off, the light and then the darkness. She doesn't think she can stand it.

"The caretaker found them."

Abdul is now crying with her, tears pouring freely down both of their faces.

"We must cable his father."

Marie thinks of the man in the photograph that Alexander showed her, comfortable, protected, with his attractive wife there in America. And now this jewel of their life gone.

She reaches up to Abdul's face and touches it, strokes his different blackness that is rich and beautiful in the darkness, and he closes his eyes.

Sometime later, it could be hours or minutes, the moth-wing now expanded fully so that time means nothing, Abdul sits across the railing of her small staircase, his back against the wall and legs fully extended, as she lies across from him on her bed. It is not really a staircase, but only what is left of one, just a few stairs to halve the space of her studio, jutting up from her wood floor. She should not have brought him here, a man in her room; eviction would be the proper punishment, but she has no thought of this.

It is as though they have traveled a long distance together, to Africa and the baobab trees she imagined when they first met—the long, hot savannahs of a continent she knows nothing about. They will wait out the long hours of the night together and then in the morning will cable Alexander's father. She does not know what they will say, how it will be possible to say anything. She watches Abdul from her bed across the room, a row of candles on the floor throwing their shadows crazily on the ceiling.

"Where is your coat?"

He does not immediately answer. "I left it with a family in the Bois de Boulogne. They were terrified. They do not know the French as I do."

Marie realizes he is speaking of the ethnographic "exhibit" at the center of the garden behind a closed gate, with tickets for admission. A group of Africans live permanently in thatched huts, for the edification and interest of passersby. It is a human zoo. There is no other word for it. The single time she went, she saw a baby playing in the dirt and children throwing food at it and laughing. A young woman caught her eye, naked from the waist up, and would not let her go. It frightened Marie so, she nearly ran home. She has not the power to imagine what those people must have felt the last few days with the rioters, or worse, whether any of them came into their compound.

Abdul looks at his hands. "Even I have been amazed by the recent actions of the French, though."

"Yes." She feels both love and hate for France right now, but does not know what she can do.

He holds out his arm and regards it in front of him. "Who am I, Marie? I do not think I know who I am."

"You are Abdul, Abdul Nadir."

"Perhaps, but I do not think so. Do you remember that day at the vineyard, when I told you about my past?"

"Yes."

"I did not tell you the truth, you know. Shall I tell you the truth now?"

"If you like." She is afraid to hear about his real past, does not think she can take anymore, but she will not show that.

He pulls his sweater higher on his neck. Marie, too, is cold and wraps her jacket more closely around her. Grief makes one cold, she thinks. She knows that from before.

"I told you my father was wealthy, yes? That was my first lie. He was a goat herder, like all my people. I would have been a goat herder too, but one day a French captain came, a tall man with a shiny sword. I was twelve, perhaps thirteen. The French had been in Senegal since my father was a boy, but mostly they did not bother us, so we did not care. Sometimes I went to their churches to see the flicker of candles. The day the captain came, my father said I must go with him. Maybe he threatened my father, maybe he paid him. I do not know."

"I am sorry."

"Do not be sorry, Marie. I thought it was a great adventure. I became a captain's boy. The French took many of us for their war with Prussia. It did not last long, but it was cold and there was much blood."

Abdul stands and walks across her room. He stoops in front of the hearth and rekindles the fire. She can feel the largeness of him kneeling in front of her bed near the fire, the space in the room that he dislodges. "I was wrong. I do not want to tell my story." He throws a piece of wood into the fire and it sparks.

"Then do not tell it." Somewhere inside her is the knowledge of what the French have done to Africa. As the candles burn down to their wicks, their shadows on the ceiling tremble, first this way, then that, in great patterns.

"Are you hungry?" she asks.

"Yes, this night has made me very hungry, I think."

Glad for a task, Marie stands and takes a pot of soup from just outside her window, to warm in the newly kindled fire. As it heats, the smell of mushrooms and cream invade her small room, and she puts out the other food she has, bread, cheese, a bit of jam. They sit across from each other at her table and finish the bread and cheese in moments. Despite what he has said, he begins to talk again.

"After the war, I wanted to go home, but the captain said no. I must go with him to Algiers. He was my father now, he said. He did not beat me, but I did not have a choice. I cried. We lived in a great stone house, like the Poussons, do you remember?" How could she not remember, Abdul huddled next to the fire, dropping the quilt when Gregoire walked in the room?

He laughs ruefully and breaks off a piece of bread. "Sometimes he dressed me in a turban and robes when his guests came, to hold his fine cognac on a silver tray like a statue. He hired women, old or young. He did not care what I saw. He wanted to know if a savage could be taught to read, so he sent me to school, when there were no other chores."

"I am sorry, Abdul." She feels tears starting again and works to hold them back.

"Do not be sorry, Marie. My story is not half so bad as many. He kept me as his unpaid servant, so yes, I was his slave, but I would not be in Paris now if not for the captain, the great captain in his fine uniform and shiny sword."

The soup starts to bubble. Marie gets it and pours out bowls for them. Though it is still dark, she can smell morning. The soup tastes so good—of mushrooms and the earth, exactly as her mother made it—and she realizes she hasn't eaten in hours. God, she is hungry. She puts the pot in the center of the table, so they can each take more as they want it. It makes her feel good to feed him this way, the way she wanted to with the food from Les Halles, as though she is putting something right.

"I also met my teacher which was a great blessing. I took his name, you know, Nadir. I had not prayed since I left my father, so we went to a great mosque and knelt together before Allah. Other days we went to a garden where the European artists came and Nadir taught me about art."

"There were so many—Renoir, an American painter named Sargent, others. That is the first time I saw a painting, and I think I fell in love, how a person could do that, take color on his brush and make life, like magic. I was grown by then. The artists heard of me in my robes and I posed for them."

At the mention of Renoir's name, Marie remembers the morning, and what she wanted to tell him. "I saw him today, Renoir. It is the last time. I told him what I thought."

Abdul nods slowly and a smile comes to his face. It is small and real, different from his flashing grin. "Good for you, Marie."

"Then I went to the Louvre and looked at paintings. I was so happy."

"Of course you were."

"And I bought something for us at Les Halles to celebrate! Well, of course I did not know that I would see you, but I wanted to." She runs to her bed, rummages in her basket for the long-forgotten raspberry tart, and unwraps it on the table. "I love them so."

They eat it in seconds with their fingers, laughing, covering themselves in crumbs.

The room is beginning to lighten and soon they will have to go to the cable office, to try to put words to what has happened, though what they will say is still beyond her. Gleyre will have the address. Perhaps he will write it. Abdul stands and walks to the window, pulling aside the curtain to watch the sunrise. She can feel a shift in the room, that he has something to tell her. He puts his hands at the small of his back and stretches.

"When I was nineteen, the Frenchman was ordered home to France. He would not take me, though. He told me to go to my father, but by then I had forgotten Senegal. I only wanted to be an artist. Nadir was a poor man, but he took me in. He said I must stay with him and be a teacher, that I could do much with my abilities, but I only thought of Paris. I worked on the docks until I had money and left."

He turns to her, the sun fully on his face, like a rainbow. "They come to me in my dreams—the captain, the American painter Sargent, the great balls he gave in his villa overlooking the sea, and behind all of them is my father, whose face I can no longer see. When I wake I think of Nadir, and all that he gave me. I should have stayed in Algiers, but when we are young, we do not know ourselves." He pauses and continues, his voice firm. "I am going home, Marie, back to Africa." He says the word as though he has not said it in decades, caressing the sound.

Something catches inside of her that makes her gasp.

His face is fully in sunlight, his back erect. "First, I will go to my parents' graves and then to Algiers, where I will live. I will be a teacher, like Nadir, and an artist. I will look for him in his courtyard, and if he is no longer alive, I will lay flowers on his grave as well.

"I am happy for you." She wants to cry, but cannot show him. Why does she feel this? He is not René, and yet it is the same feeling, like drowning, like going blind, opening to him and losing him at the same moment. She feels her face start to crack. He moves to her, holding her head and smoothing her hair.

"Do not be sad, Marie. If it were not for Alexander, I would be happy, for the first time in so long."

"I know."

"You will visit me, yes? It is not so far."

"Of course." She thinks of the Algerian courtyards and blankets of bougainvillea that she has seen in paintings, the turquoise water and ancient alleys. In the mornings, they will drink their coffees overlooking the sea. "And you will visit me in Paris?"

"Many times. Your paintings shall hang in the Luxemburg, in great golden frames. I will say that I knew you when we were both students, and I will be proud."

X

She stands in the wagon, driving the horse through her father's fields, the wheat above the wagon wheels. She is blinded by the yellow fields, everywhere around her, close to his house now, and each kilometer she draws nearer, her fear grows, no longer the fear of Renoir, but of the life she left behind. If Abdul could go home, so could she; it was less a decision than a compulsion, her two friends gone, Paris empty without them, and the work with Renoir over for good. She stayed just long enough to greet Alexander's father as he stepped off the train, a neat gray man in a cravat and worsted suit, who took her for dinner at a great chandeliered hotel to thank her for being his son's friend. His hands were the same, she could not stop thinking that, the way he kept smoothing the tablecloth and repositioning his knife, as though the grief inside of him could ever be contained. He ordered lamb chops, champagne, spoke to the waiters in impeccable French. His eyes were Alexander's, although his hair was dark. Neither of them really ate. She asked him where Alexander's red hair came from, and though he answered his wife, he looked at her with such pain, that she knew not to say anything else.

The next few days she spent in her room, only hot and dull, and then without thinking, she rented the wagon with the remainder of her money from Renoir and left.

And now she can see the house on the horizon, the exact house of her childhood— why should it have changed? the trees the same, the dog—like stepping back through layers of memory, to this place where she was a different person, only here she is today. Even the horse knows where to go, walking himself toward the barn.

It is so quiet, that is the first thing she thinks, quiet and serene. Of course, no one is there. Off in the distance is a small cloud of dust, where she knows her father is clearing land.

She pushes open the door and is hit by the sweet smell and familiarity of the house, old wood well-cured in the beams. This was her life, this room and the two next to it. Her brothers, before they married, slept in a shack off the barn. After their marriages, the father could have lived with them but he refused. It was assumed, René now dead and her mother gone, that she would care for him, but then she didn't. What future could have grown from this? she asks Abdul in her mind. She passes her father's room, the door ajar, a white throw loosely covering a bed by a window. "This is where my father slept."

In the next room, her old bed and other things are pushed in a corner, the blue and white ticking of the mattress half-covered with old clothes. "And where René and I slept when he was alive." *And where he died*, she thinks but does not say. The conversation keeps things at bay. She tries to imagine Abdul in Algiers as he described it, turquoise skies and blinding white streets. If she can, she will buy a ticket to go in the winter. He will not be so hard to find, an African from Paris teaching art.

A great fatigue comes over her. She pushes some things off the mattress, lies down, and is asleep in moments. When she wakes, it is dusk, her father standing in the doorway. She senses he has been there for a while. As she sits up, he nods and goes to the other room, neither of them speaking. It is clear from the nod that he believes she has returned for good. He is older, though not by much, the patches of his red beard still bright on his face, his skin more mottled by the sun.

"And this is my father," she says, but the trick no longer works, so much guilt inside of her for leaving, but also anger at all of them for what they said.

In the main room, he is sitting in his chair, waiting as he waited each night for her mother to cook his meal. So this is why she has come home, she thinks ruefully, but acquiesces. If not, what would they eat? Besides, he is old and it is the least she can do. She finds a few fresh vegetables in a cupboard and some cured sausages, the kind he has always loved. It is hardly enough for one person, but she'll add rice, other things. It is clear he has lost weight and is not eating enough.

Throughout dinner he says nothing and she does not break the silence. Only his eyes watch her when he thinks she isn't looking.

"You have come home," he finally says, as she is clearing the table.

She waits a long time before answering. "Yes, to visit. I am not staying. How have you been, Father?" She pours him his evening coffee.

He also waits before answering. "Your place is here." There is no anger in his voice, only need.

"Yes, I know, but I live in Paris now. It is not so far. I will visit often. I am an artist now." Her eldest brother lives on a farm not so far away and has done well for himself. They have made a room for him that he refuses to go to; it is only his stubbornness, like her stubbornness, she realizes. She gives him one of the sweet rolls he loves from the oven. All at once, she feels such love for him, she does not know where it comes from. Bending over him, she kisses his forehead, and he closes his eyes.

She stays a month in Normandy, long enough to cook mushroom soup several times and to see all her brothers who welcome her. Even René's sister comes, who still does not embrace her, though her eyes are soft when she looks at Marie and she takes her hand. The next day, she visits René's grave. The pain is so fresh there, and now combined with the pain from Alexander, the two together. She does not run from it, though. She stays for a long time. Before she leaves, she finds daffodils growing wild and sets them on the grave.

Now, back in Paris, it is early summer, and she feels herself to be changed. In the few short months since Abdul left, she is no longer so thin. Too much good food, first in Normandy and then with Gabrielle and Gregoire, she decides, but really it is as though something inside of her has opened. Her life is hardly different, modeling for Valadon, other artists, but she is messier with herself, her hair hanging loose, her dresses open. She laughs more and drinks more champagne. A few of her canvases lean against the wall in this private sunroom that the Poussons have given her, figures and landscapes in bright, open colors. They are just rehearsals, though. This is the real painting, *Women Bathing*, that she first imagined in the museum gallery and has waited so long to paint.

To make the scene, she has placed a porcelain tub in an alcove of windows, looking out onto a private spot in the garden. Gabrielle luxuriates in the water, her smile and nicely rounded belly open to the viewer's eye. She holds a champagne glass to the window that catches a ray of light and laughs. Valadon sits across from her on the edge of the porcelain, one leg raised, her nearing middle-aged body and breasts unashamed to reveal themselves. It is a harem, the two of them, that Marie is creating. It fits how she feels. Occasionally Valadon puffs on a short cigar, drinks from her glass, says something funny, returns to the pose.

She layers the paint quickly in bold strokes and blocks of color. There is a teenager from Barcelona, Valadon says, who sits in the cafés all night talking incessantly about how he will reinvent art, and how he will be the most famous artist of the twentieth century. He says there is no one single vision to the form; that the artist must communicate all points of view. He calls it Cubism.

A maid walks in to refresh the hot water, though it is a warm day and Gabrielle has not complained. From the back of the house, Marie can hear footfalls and male laughter, and thinks with excitement of the evening ahead and the other guests that will join them. The old electricity she would have next to a man has returned, the quickening and the brightness. Behind the laughter are smells of the meal that invade the sunroom and make her hungry.

"And have you seen this young man's work?" Marie asks. She lifts her bare calf onto a chair, dips into a puddle of red on her palette, and deftly outlines the window behind them. She was so precise before in her work, things took forever, which was Gleyre's major criticism, but now all that is gone. She works for gesture and form, and will decide later on exact placement. She drinks from her champagne, sketches more. It is difficult for Marie to imagine the teenager's work. She knows, though, that Renoir's absurd perfection of the female form will only garner criticism in the years to come. She thinks the surface of the canvas should be as real as the subject, alive with color and texture, like Van Gogh or Gauguin.

"Not yet. He talks all night about how great he is but shows no one."

Marie cannot imagine what such art would look like, from all points of view, though likes the idea immediately.

"If I were an artist, I would paint only birds, like that small bird outside the window," Gabrielle says, pointing to a tiny sparrow just hopping onto a branch. All of them are stopped for a moment by the beauty of the bird, the streaks of red in its delicate wings and its golden beak. "I think, though, that it is enough to simply know nature and observe it. I have begun a diary of birds, you know."

"You have? I want very much to see it. We must illustrate it. And there are many books on the subject." Marie is excited to think her friend has found her vocation.

Gabrielle laughs. "It is nothing as serious as you imagine, Marie. For now, I am well satisfied to observe the life in my body and all the world around me."

As she speaks, Gabrielle looks different to Marie, older, more confident. They are quiet for a time, with only her brush on the canvas and the sounds of the house to disturb them. The smells of their dinner grow richer and she knows that soon, it will be time to stop for the day and enter what awaits her.

"Women Bathing" is inspired by the later works of Auguste Renoir and the history of the Dreyfus Affair. While scenes with the artist are fictional, his comments about women and Jews, and the comments of other Impressionist artists, are based on fact, as are the comments of the Viennese journalist Theodor Herzl, called by some the father of Zionism.

Vermeer's Light

I

My new friend Abe is a sweet married man in his forties who shoots furniture for Sears catalogues, and does art photography on the side. He is not happy with his life, he has told me this. He says his existence is a facade, and that everything he does is for appearance. He wishes he were famous, or at least made more money. I know Abe because our studios have shared the same floor in a loft building in downtown Los Angeles for the last three years; I am a painter—also not famous, but as a woman I am allowed the indulgence of my art. I am divorced, a big difference between us, though I try not to think about this.

Abe and I don't always talk about personal things, but if we did I wouldn't mind. We have tea every day at four, before he leaves and I go to work, unless it's a weekend, as it is today; then we meet earlier. There is a kindness about Abe, almost a transparency, that is very appealing. It is as though he's aware of how vulnerable the world is, and he is walking across it gently, so as not to hurt all the living things underneath.

"Did you know," I say, filling an old pot with water to boil for our tea, "that Johannes Vermeer, the great Dutch painter, went almost unrecognized in his lifetime?" I am giving Abe a pep talk, because I think he needs it: keep doing your own work, it's the quality that counts. "People knew he was an artist, he wasn't overlooked like Van Gogh, but that almost makes it worse. People knew about his work, even went to his art exhibits, but decided it wasn't very good.

I've been reading a lot about Vermeer; I'm not sure why. Abe is standing at the far end of my loft, looking out the window at the downtown Los Angeles street below. But when I turn to see if he is listening, I see instead his face washed out with light, his prematurely gray hair shining in the sun. Though we have only been meeting like this for a couple of weeks, I am already building my days around these afternoons, wondering what to talk about, and how to keep him with me longer. At the same time, I argue with myself: Put your number in a personals ad, get out and meet single men, what are you doing? You're getting old. You've been divorced five years, and you've barely gone out.

"Isn't he the one who painted all the portraits of women?" he asks, raising his eyebrows and looking interested. He is asking out of politeness. He sticks his hands in the pockets of his faded blue jeans, and walks over to help me with the tea—to carry the tray to my table and set out biscuits. Abe humors me this way, which is another reason why I like him.

"Yes—you remember—the one of the lady in blue, standing by the window, reading a letter. Here:

I open a book of Vermeer. The colored plates flicker past, small and distant in their thick paper frames, and then I come to the one we are talking about: *Woman in Blue Reading a Letter*, 1662–64. We both stare at it a moment, feeling the Dutch sun on our faces, the mystery of the letter in the young woman's hand.

"Almost nothing is known about him," I continue. "Literally— no records were kept. Art historians go nuts about it. They know he was in a local painters' guild, and he made some money off odd commissions. But that's it. Really. More records were kept on his mother-in-law."

Abe's studio and mine have occupied the same floor of this building for the last three years; we would nod to each other, but that was all. Then one day I was carrying some equipment up on the elevator and he was with me, and I asked him to hold open my front door. This too could have gone by unnoticed; Abe is that way, a man who can slip between cracks, pass unseen in large crowds, but that day I saw him, and when I had put my packages down, I offered to make us some tea. While I was boiling the water, smelling the chamomile drift up through the brown paper wrapping, he stood quietly and looked at my paintings, the small abstract expressionist canvases that I make in my time off from teaching at a local college.

We'd had a tenants' meeting that Abe had missed, and I was telling him about it. I turned around to see if he was listening, but what I saw instead was his gentle face and gray hair, framed by the blue of the open sky.

"Are you going to the meeting tonight?" I ask.

"I'm not sure," he says. "I'll have to see when I get home."

He takes the handle of the teapot, and I think, *What attractive hands, warm and dry, nails like clean shells.* The hot brown liquid splashes into our cups.

Like most painters, I keep little furniture in my loft—a couch, a chair, a bookcase with the lamps and other things that I collect. When oil paint gets wet, it smells of linseed oil and turpentine, pungent odors that mix with the trance of art-making, so you don't know afterwards if you've gotten high off the smells or the art, or both. The smell, combined with the vivid colors of the paint, has always been enough for me. I don't like distractions. I think of myself as a woman who likes to be alone.

"Did you see the new girl?" I offer. "The one who moved in with her boyfriend?"

Abe grins.

"Not so bad," he says.

"Ya, if you like beautiful bodies and incredibly thin waists."

She is actually a messy art-student type with too many rings on her fingers, and a large tattoo of a parrot on her neck. She probably calls herself a "conceptual artist," or maybe she does "performance art." She'll get out her old tampons and swing them red and bloody from a hanger, and some art critic will call it important. She and her boyfriend were moving in, and I saw her just as I stepped off the elevator. She was wearing old bell bottoms, dirty and ripped from the sixties with a teensy halter top. I was ready to say hello, be polite, but she ignored me. She was chewing gum and laughing with him, their music blaring.

"It's the parties I'm worried about," I say. "Her boyfriend's a goddamn musician —from Prague no less."

"If there's any trouble I'll talk to them. This is a working building. They won't want to make enemies."

"Why do kids like that come here anyway?"

"Maybe they want to be artists."

We talk on about a few other things, but I know our tea is over. I see it in the lengthening shadows on my wall, the slanted rays of light from the skylight above.

Abe looks at me. His eyes are gray/blue, and sometimes we look too long at each other, stare too much into each other's eyes, which is what is happening now. It is our little pretense, as though we were not both forty years old, one married, the other divorced.

"You know, in each of Vermeer's paintings, the light is coming from the same window at the left-hand side of the canvas. The room is the same in each one too, the checkered floor, the tapestry on the far wall. Like he did them all in the same place. . .Do you want something to eat? I'm sorry I didn't get anything."

"No. . .That's all right." Abe stands.

Don't go, I think, but it is too late.

When he's gone, I pick up the book again, and look for the lady in blue. She seems pregnant, though this may only have been the style of dress. There is a mystery about this painting, of course, the letter she is reading: Who is it from? What is it about? I have always assumed it was from her lover, though art historians disagree. The light of Delft is suffusing her face, shining through the pages of the letter, and Vermeer has painted this light as though we can literally touch it.

There is a knock at the door and when I go to answer it is the girl.

"I'm Ricky Jones," she says, stepping into my loft without being asked.

She puts her hand in my face, and there is nothing to do but shake it. Up close she is tall and bony, and younger than I thought, no more than nineteen or twenty.

"Julia Stein."

Her nails, painted gold and chipped, are bitten to the quick. The other things I notice are that she has a nose ring, and she is very tan. The large patch of skin between her bell bottoms and halter top is dark and completely flat.

"I thought I should introduce myself. We just moved in."

She strides into the center of the room, stopping beneath my skylights. My loft is the tallest in the building, and also has the best light, which is why I took it. Even though it is close to sundown, there is still a lot of light. She closes her eyes in a patch of orange sun, her delicate chin pointing to the sky. In spite of the disruption, I have to admit she looks beatific, like a young Saint Teresa, beautiful enough to paint.

"Sun is great, don't you think? Do you ever sunbathe here?"

"No."

"You should. I have this great coconut oil from Mexico. We were in Mexico on vacation. Jan—that's my boyfriend—he loved it. You could borrow it if you want."

She comes to, then notices a row of my paintings against the wall. I've been working on a series of small red canvases, thick strokes of paint layered over and over and though I don't quite know where the paintings are going, I like them.

"I make sculpture," she smiles. "Plastic." She holds up one of the paintings and turns it sideways. "Nice, but you're not using this space."

She twirls around and around, her arms outstretched as though to show the space to me, doing a little jig on her cowboy boots and humming to herself. When she finally finishes she moves toward the door: "You'll have to come over and see my stuff. My boyfriend's a bass player —sometimes we get a little loud. Bang on the door, OK?"

"Have you decided about the tenants' meeting tonight?" I ask Abe over the telephone. "You should come."

The girl has unnerved me, and I want to hear his voice again, the gentle stillness of it, so this is my excuse to call. I have used the number he has given me for emergencies. He does not live in his studio, but in the hills of Hollywood, in a too-expensive white house that I have not seen but he has told me about. It has porticoes, and a small pool in the backyard. He only talks briefly to me on the phone—in a very distant and business-like tone—but listening to him calms me. He says that he will come. So this will be new for us—a rendezvous in true darkness—and to celebrate the possibilities I take a bath, slip into a silk blouse, splash on cologne.

I know I shouldn't have fantasies about Abe, but it's hard not to. While I'm in the bath my mind slips into an imagination of him, his reserve dissolving, pinning me against the wall of my loft in a wild embrace, the wildness directly opposite to the degree of his inner restraint. Then I imagine we are on a long bus ride. We are traveling somewhere, maybe going to another city to look at art—and the bus stops, and we step off together in the sound of the closing mufflers and squealing brakes.

He takes my hand, and leads me to the edge of a cornfield that butts up against the parking lot.

"Let's get off the bus and stay the night," he says.

There is a new hardness in him, a firmness, and I see it in the set of his expression, the way he holds my hand, completely sure of himself. The side of the bus glints in the late afternoon light. The hair under Abe's collar is dark, and I think of what his chest must look like, darker still.

He brushes the side of my cheek gently with his hand. "We could get a motel room," he says.

He says it simply, but there is so much underneath. I think of how his body will feel, his lips—soft. Will this be the beginning of our new life? Dinner twice a week, sex? We can take care of each other. I don't think about marriage and divorce. But the fact is, Abe told me about his marriage the first day we had tea. He was sitting on my couch, talking about the painters he admired—Turner, Eakins, Sargent—and he carefully interjected the word "wife" into all his sentences: "My wife and I go to Europe every year to look at museums." "My wife likes this painter or that." A few days later I saw her—a pointy woman driving a dust-free, dark green Acura. She is compact, with short hair and a perfectly tanned and exercised body. We are the same age, I am sure, but aging in different ways: the unmistakable signs are on her dark and wrinkled face, whereas mine are on my body.

I knew nothing about her and had no reason to dislike her, but I worried immediately that she was wrong for him. She is a television producer and from what I could gather makes the lion's share of their income, or at least enough to discourage Abe's fantasies of being a successful photographer. I wanted to yell at her, and at Abe for following her: "What do you need all that money for? The Acura, the large house? You have no children. Who are you trying to impress?"

He seemed sad when he told me about his wife, looked away quickly, and then back again to make sure I hadn't left him, that I would stay with him through the conversation, my eyes into his, as long as was necessary. And why should I leave him? A handsome man sitting on my couch, talking into the late afternoon. Like most of our teas together, the afternoon began stretching into evening, my loft darkening, neither of us getting up to turn on a light.

Will Abe's wife accompany him to the tenants' meeting, or will he come alone?

This is the question of the hour, and I think about it obsessively as I straighten my magazines, drink a glass of wine to calm my nerves. There are still a few minutes left before I must meet everyone on the first floor, and I have never been good at waiting, especially when something good might happen. I read in a magazine recently that sometimes women who have trouble with relationships—who haven't really been able to trust men—can change this completely with a married man. While this might sound ridiculous, the article made it seem reasonable. Because the relationship is limited, the woman feels safe, and can therefore reach her deepest feelings. So, I am ready. I will go along with whatever happens.

I turn out my lights and open the door. Instead of seeing the thin strip of light under Abe's door, though, I see the girl and her boyfriend, standing in the hallway, drinking beer with a friend and playing music. The boyfriend is a shockingly handsome young man, as good looking as a fashion model, very tall and blond, with a naked chest and heavy cowboy boots, and she is wearing a see-through, sequined dress.

Before I know what has happened, he has grabbed me and put his arm around me.

"Hello Julia Stein!" he yells in a deep, Czechoslovakian accent.

He puts a cold beer in my hand. "Ricky says you're a painter."

"Yes!"

"That's great! I'm Jan. Jan is bass player!" He laughs, a laugh that is thoroughly contented with itself, with life, with art. His arm around me is sweaty and hot, and for a moment I am shocked into the realness of his body, into how long it's been since I've been with a man. Suddenly he lets go and stumbles into his loft. Though the evening is young, he is very drunk.

"Jan am bass player!!!"

He slides on his knees Mick-Jagger style to the center of the room and pounds on his naked chest, then picks up a bass guitar, and strums it, making a terrible, grating noise. This does not fully describe the scene, though. We have all turned to watch him - myself, Ricky, the other young man, who looks a bit preppie, as though he might be a filmmaker, or a young lawyer on the slum—and what we see when we turn is truly extraordinary: Jan kneeling in the center of the darkened room like a young Saint Sebastian, pounding and strumming, and all around him, hanging from the ceiling, are Ricky's sculptures: diaphanous angel wings, made of clear plastic, and edged in pink.

II

There are dozens of people at the tenants' meeting when I arrive. Our landlord owns three buildings, and most of the people are here—some sitting on the floor, the latecomers lining the walls.

There are all types—painters, filmmakers, writers—some scruffy and punk, others looking like young executives on their day off. You think you can categorize artists, but then when you're with so many at once, you realize you can't. The only defining feature is age; the majority are under thirty-five. It's not that the desire to be an artist ever wanes in people; it's just that life takes over. A window is open at the side of the room, and the night sky is coming in very blue, a few stars just visible.

I find a place on the floor, and am scanning the crowd, when I see Abe walk in, alone, and take a place against the wall. Our eyes meet immediately. My knees are pinned under my chest, and I can smell myself: Jan's sweat, my own perfume. I can feel my heart flutter.

"So, we have this agenda," someone is saying. I look toward the front of the room and see an intense young man of about thirty, short and dark, a good choice to lead this group. He is a computer animator who used to be a lawyer; his name is Zeke. I know him because he has a loft on the second floor. Zeke waves a little scrap of paper above his head and tries to keep our focus, but already small groups have begun to form, talking boisterously.

He reads quickly and loud: "Plumbing in the building on 4th Street; miscellaneous earthquake renovations; and an item from last time—courtesy of the girls down the block—he grins at a row of girls who are sitting in front—"which is a revolving gallery on the first floor of Bates Street. I don't know about the rest of you, but I'd like to do something else tonight, so let's get going."

The meeting proceeds, but I only half listen. I keep my eyes on Zeke but my head turned to the side, so that Abe is just at the edge of my vision. Around me people laugh, argue, then laugh again. A young man stands up, demanding to hold elections, but he is booed down. Finally, it's over. Because the landlord must fix plumbing and make earthquake repairs, a few young men volunteer to negotiate with his office and, if need be, check our legal status should we need to hold a rent strike. The girls down the block will present a formal proposal at next month's meeting.

The meeting adjourns and I am bunched up in a large group near the door, when Abe begins to move toward me. I realize he will sense my warmth, see the redness of my lipstick, and the way my hair shines under the light. Maybe he will even smell me.

"Hi," he says.

"Hi."

We are standing by the elevator, waiting for it to go down to street level, then back up. I feel like I can't talk. I am thinking/hoping that anything might happen now, that at the very least he will invite me out for coffee. A sweet warmth is rising up from my breasts, and I can feel their softness against my arm. Abe is silent. I wonder if I should make the first move—after all I'm a liberated woman. The hallway is a colorless steel metal gray, and my silk magenta blouse stands out against it in high relief. The elevator clangs back up and opens.

"I have to go back up and get a camera," he says, and both of us step on.

When you haven't been with someone for a long time, you worry how things will be; if they'll go all right. Many people step onto the elevator with us, but aside from Abe and myself, there might as well be no one. We both stare straight ahead, don't talk. I feel like we are encased in glass.

My last relationship did not go well. It was over two years ago. He was a doctor in his late forties, who supervised a pediatric intensive care unit at a major hospital. He had a house in Malibu and a BMW, but our affair did not last long. It was not so much an affair, really, as a few weekends stretched out over several months, and some very intense sex.

Finally, I told him to leave me alone, because I got tired of all the rejection. He would seduce me with long-stemmed red roses, and trips to Santa Barbara, and then, when we'd finally made love, had our single night of intimacy and passion, tell me that he loved someone else. I wouldn't hear from him for a month or two, and all of a sudden it would begin again—the trips, the apologies, the declarations of love. For a while I kept the roses hanging from my ceiling, drying them upside down to preserve their buds. By the end I had five bouquets.

The third floor is pitch black when we step off the elevator, and it takes a moment for our eyes to adjust. Someone has unscrewed the bulb from the ceiling. At the same time there is loud noise and music coming from Ricky and Jan's loft, and vague bodies brushing past us in the dark. Abe cups his hand under my elbow to guide me through the maze, but halfway there a door bursts open, spilling out light. In the center of it is Jan, backlit and grinning. He pulls each one of us inside, and kisses me on both cheeks. "Zo glad you kud make it," he clowns, in an exaggerated Dracula accent.

He shuts the door so we cannot leave. A party is in full swing, people dancing, other groups laughing and talking, sprouted in corners like young trees. This is the noise I was worried about, but somehow, with Abe next to me, I don't mind it so much; in fact, it makes my blood rise.

"I really can't stay," Abe is saying. "I have to go."

He looks amused, but it's impossible to know what he is really thinking. He is only a few feet away, and I feel his presence like a block of heat. I shake out my blouse, watch the magenta silk fall in folds around my bracelets.

"Wine, beer. . .?" Jan bows to a long table at the side of the room, already covered with empty bottles, busted kegs, spilled cups.

"Thank you anyway."

Someone opens a bottle of champagne, and a loud bang goes off. An accordion player—later I learn he is Jan's friend from Czechoslovakia—moves to the center of the room and starts to play. His music is a mix of Czechoslovakian folk singing and rock, and it is electrifying. Jan cups his hand over Abe's ear and shouts something; Abe smiles and shrugs.

A circle forms around the accordion player—tight, excited, people stomping with the music and laughing. He is a wild, middle-aged man with peppery gray hair and a cherubic face, and his fingers fly up and down the keys of his accordion as he growls out his lyrics, shouting them into our faces Kafka-like. A few people move into the center of the circle and start to dance. I love to dance. When I was young I could stay up all night dancing; and even now when I hear good music, something inside me moves and I have to get out on the floor. I think about dancing, with Abe watching, wonder if I could. I turn to look for him. Jan has led him to a bookcase and is showing him an antique camera. So, for the moment, he is absorbed. His slender fingers touch the camera gently, pointing out this part or that. For the moment, he is not going to leave.

I turn back. The song is moving to a crescendo now, and as it does, I step out onto the floor. I haven't danced in years, and at first it comes slowly, but then, all of a sudden, my hands are above my head and I feel the music inside me, everything moving in unison. For a while I am only inside the music, and then I remember Abe.

My eyes half-closed, I spin around to find him. He is at the edge of the circle, turned toward the door, but he isn't leaving. He has his hands in his jeans, the way he did at my window. His feet are tapping lightly, and he is looking at me—only at me—his gray/blue eyes shining, a big, slow grin on his face.

"How did you meet Jan?" I ask.

It is now very late, probably past three; Abe left hours ago. We shared a glass of wine, and he kissed me on the cheek, and then he said goodbye. So now Ricky and I are cruising the streets of east Hollywood in her ancient VW, looking for an all-night supermarket; we are hunting down breakfast supplies. It is a futile and dangerous exercise, I tell her, neither of us know the area. In fact, I'm not even sure why I've come. I feel young and ridiculous.

"It was in Prague last year," she says. "It was great. His band was playing at this little club, and afterwards I hung around so I could meet him. Jimmy was there too." Jimmy is the accordion player.

It rained earlier, and the streetlights throw little pools of light on the wet pavement.

"Prague's exciting, you know. There's a lot happening. You should go."

As she talks about Prague, I picture the city: full of Western entrepreneurs, American students, Czech rebels, everyone trying to make a better life. It's getting overrun, she says. But somewhere in a dark alley, the old stones must still exist; calls of a foreign language; the lure of the medieval. The night she met Jan, he took her to one of those alleys. He was practically homeless, flopping on someone's couch, so they didn't really have a place to go—and they did it up against a car, the sounds of Prague drifting in and out, like the cats at their feet. She was on a college tour and already seeing two other boys, but after that it was clear.

"He was like no one I'd ever met before," she explains. When the tour was over, she went back, and together they waited out the six months for his visa.

A supermarket looms ahead, its blue-white fluorescents pulsing against the sky.

"How did you meet Abe?"

"Oh, we're not a couple," I say too quickly.

"You sure seem like one—did you see the way he was looking at you?"

I grin: "He's married, for Christ's sake!"

"So? If it's meant to be, it's meant to be. Do you like him?" She looks at me pointedly.

"Yes."

"Jan had a girlfriend, you know. They were going to get married. They were even almost engaged!"

It has now been three days since the party—since the shared glass of wine and good-night kiss—and I have not seen Abe. Two days ago, he left a message saying he was in the desert, and not to expect him till the end of the week. To give myself a mission, I went to the library and checked out a few books on Vermeer, even a video. I want to surprise him—show him my find—which I will do, since he is coming today.

It is close to sundown when he finally shows up, though, tired and dusty from the long drive. I let the books sit between us on the table, the cover portrait of Vermeer's *Girl with a Red Hat* lost and forgotten.

He sits down, and pours the tea. "How have you been?" I ask.

"Good, yourself?"

He says it quickly, trying not to meet my gaze. He gets tripped up, though, when he has to hand me the cup of tea. Then he has to look at me, and when he looks at me, he looks into my eyes. His face reddens. I take the teacup and tuck my legs under me.

"Their party was something, wasn't it?"

He raises his eyebrows: "The noise didn't seem to bother you."

"No, I guess it didn't!"

The three-day absence has given us breathing space, a chance to feel ourselves again, and at the same time things are heightened, nervous, like you're balanced on the end of a pin, and you don't know which way you're going to fall. I feel flushed. I want to stare only at the center of his chest, at his gray wool sweater, imagining what it would be like to lay my head there, to feel the slow rise and fall of his chest, to smell him. He is sitting on my couch, in the center of it, so there would be plenty of room—lying on my side, my head in his lap.

"Do you like my new lamp?" I ask.

I jump up and turn on a small tulip lamp that I've just picked up from the repairman. It has metal branches rising from the base, and each branch is studded with tiny tulip bulbs sprouted beneath green plastic leaves. It will be part of my collection of lamps—from the forties and fifties—that I keep on the wall above my paints.

"I got it at a garage sale. It was only a few bucks."

"Nice."

We talk on about other things; I don't keep track: points about the tenants' meeting, a question about my painting, "Oh the tea is delicious!" "Yes, I got it at a new store."

Abe turns his wrist and looks at his watch: beautiful watch, gold nestled in thin silver hairs. "Time to go," he says. He stands.

I stand with him: "I want to say something," I say, not knowing I would say this, but now that I have the die is cast.

"Yes?"

The flush moves to my stomach. I follow him to the door, so we are opposite each other, close.

"I want to say...that I really like you," I say. "I like you a lot." For the smallest moment his eyes dilate and a smile of pleasure washes across his face, and then the next moment his head tilts, and his eyes close Geisha-like.

"I like you too," he says, and hugs me—warm, brotherly—surrounding me in a soft cloud of gray.

The door closes. It clicks, a heavy metal sound, like a key turning in a well-greased lock. Then I am alone; under my skylight, alone.

I stand like that for several seconds, unsure of what to do, unsure about how things will work out, above all unsure about the hug. I crawl into bed, my clothes on, tucking the blanket under my chin. Things might work out, of course, but somehow—now—I don't think so. It has happened before. The first time I fell in love, I was twenty-two, not much older than Ricky is now. He was an actor, already in his thirties, and when he kissed me, I literally heard bells.

I turned my head in an aura of perfume and clean hair, and then there he was, his lips, the bells, and I said to myself, *This is what they mean about hearing bells.*

After three months, he moved to San Francisco, went back to an old girlfriend, but that first night we couldn't get each other's clothes off fast enough, left them scattered in a trail behind us, insignificant pieces of color on the way to heaven. Later in bed as I held his face between my hands, he looked so beautiful to me— glowing and pink from the lamp by my bed— and I said that over and over, "beautiful, beautiful, beautiful," and I kissed him.

Shortly after Abe's visit, I hear from someone in the building that he is leaving. There are a few intermittent teas, but it is essentially over. I bump into him by the dumpsters, and when I ask why he explains that he isn't making enough to support a studio, which is basically true. He will work out of his garage.

Since it's hard to see myself as the cause, I accept his story at face value. If I am somehow involved, it is only coincidentally, like killing two birds with one stone—an English expression I have always abhorred. Whenever I use the phrase, I picture the stone hurtling through the air—the two birds in their nest—feathers flying, shrieking squawks everywhere.

The very last time I see Abe I am going down for mail. The mailman has left, and I am sifting through junk mail and bills, when a dark green Acura pulls into the lot. Immediately I am afraid of being spotted, and push into a corner behind the plate-glass door, and yet at the same time I don't want to leave; I want to watch everything. Abe is sitting in the passenger seat, his arm out the window, the back seat full of boxes and old rolls of paper. A diagonal strip of shadow is falling across his closed eyes, and I want to reach out to him, brush the shadow away, but I don't know how. I hear the sound of high heels on pavement, someone rummaging through boxes, and then the trunk slams shut and a thin, tanned calf walks back to the driver's seat, climbs in and drives away. And as the car dwindles in the distance, a familiar wave of nausea opens up inside of me, opens up into nothing.

"What is 'nothing'?" I asked my eighth-grade science teacher once, in the middle of his lesson on astronomy and galaxies. Everything is something; the space between the galaxies may be vast, thin, without oxygen, but it exists.

Or take a painting—a head on a white canvas. My beginners at school make this mistake all the time: They forget the background, the whiteness behind their portraits. They'll spend hours on their pictures—replicating every eyelash, the pouting lips, gold and green flecks of the iris, and then when it's done it's still swimming in a field of white, just as I am swimming now— watching the car drive away, the point of green dissolving into white smog and oncoming cars.

III

"Knock, knock...anybody home?"

I have left my door ajar. It is a mistake, since I want to feel sorry for myself now; I want to cry. When I turn, I see Ricky and Jan, though, standing in the doorjamb like children, a tray of brownies in Ricky's hand. Jan has peroxided his hair white, and it is shaved up the back in a Mohawk.

"Can we come in?" Ricky asks, her voice little and high.

Not waiting for my answer, they both proceed inside, Ricky walking toward me with the brownies, Jan exploring the loft; he makes a beeline for the small stack of canvases I keep against a far wall.

"I made these," she says. "No, they do not have marijuana in them, Jan's mother—she's still in Prague, you know, in this little house—she gave me the recipe. They call them something else; they're incredible!"

Ricky jumps up on a kitchen stool, picking into the brownies with her fingers. She pulls out a large square, eating the chocolate from the bottom; the chocolate icing dangles in a thin thread.

"You should have a show," Jan calls from the other side of the room. "These are really good."

"Do you have anything to drink?" Ricky asks, her mouth

smudged with chocolate. "We're out of milk. We feel bad about the other night; about being so loud. Our first night and everything."

I open the refrigerator. "It was fine."

"Really?"

"It was good for me."

I set a quart in front of her, then take down a kettle for tea, and get out my cups. Perhaps this will become my new ritual, I think, tea with a couple of twenty-year-olds. There isn't a third cup, so I add a jelly glass. They drink tea in Russia that way, in little jelly glasses, the square of sugar held tight between their teeth. Maybe they also do in Czechoslovakia.

Jan takes a seat on the other stool. "So, Abe left," he says.

Ricky pokes him in the ribs.

"Yes." I set out a box of sugar.

"He was an idiot," he says. "I saw his wife."

"You can't judge people from the outside," I tell them. "You don't know what's really going on."

When Ricky and Jan leave, I pour a second cup of tea, and settle onto the couch. It is the time of day Abe would be dropping by, and it is hard not to think about him. The orange light from the skylight bathes my outstretched legs, as though I might be on Ricky's beach in Mexico, smelling coconut oil and flirting with boys.

Before I met Abe, I hadn't liked anyone in a long time; so, maybe I should be glad, maybe this is a first step back. I lie down and try to sleep, dream about something. When I wake, it is past dinnertime, but I am not hungry. I pick up one of the books about Vermeer and run my hand across the cover. According to the book jacket, the writer is a curator of Northern Baroque painting at the National Gallery of Art in Washington. What must that be like, to come to work every day at the National Gallery? Their storerooms would be crowded with impasto canvases, cool, perfectly humidified for conservation. Would he wander through them, running his fingers across the ornate gold frames, or is he a modern curator, who holds lunch meetings with his assistants over pasta salads and Pinot Noir, and dresses in Italian suits?

I turn on a lamp and open the book. The introduction begins slowly, as these books always do: descriptions of seventeenth-century

Delft, the social and commercial life of Holland, illustrations of a city, a house, a map. Everything is conjecture, of course; there is almost no information. Even the dates of his paintings are guesswork: 1662–1665, *The Music Lesson* (A Lady at the Virginals with a Gentleman); 1664, *Woman with a Pearl Necklace*; 1662–1664, *A Woman Holding a Balance.* (In this last, the most mysterious, a young woman holds an empty measure, weighing some decision of her soul, while her jewelry lies before her on a table.)

Is it a coincidence that all of Vermeer's women look the same, the writer asks—and in addition to being posed in the same room, wear identical, yellow dresses trimmed in fur? Aside from the woman in blue, this in fact becomes the trademark, the identifying feature: fifteen years of delicate blond matrons—at music lessons, at mirrors, some reading letters, others writing them; the one ambiguous scene of the scale: "The woman does not appear tempted by the jewels," the curator explains, ". . .her attitude is one of inner peace." A later painting, *The Love Letter*, shows the now-aging matron, interrupted at her music, as she hands a sealed letter to her maid.

As I read, it slowly dawns on me—the answer to the puzzle. It makes sense if you take the paintings out of sequence, a few chronological, but most dipping back into the artist's memory, as memory always does. First there is the girl, then the young woman: practicing at her concertina, her teacher beside her. In another painting, she is dreaming serenely, while an emblem above warns that "Love requyres sinceritie"; and then the first letter, received in front of the open window, to be followed by so many more.

That first day he met her, did he put his leathered boot on the floor of her house and feel like an ugly oaf in comparison to her, his art student, perhaps, or the young wife of a patron? She was clearly rich, with her pearl earrings and fur-trimmed clothing; he could never have offered her that. When was it that he conceived of the paintings at the window? The first came in 1657, five years after his own marriage, so the conflict was clear. If he could not touch her skin in fact, he would touch it in light, bathe it in light; write her letters which she would read in secret, and through the thin pages of his letters, the light alone would surround her.

Each of Vermeer's days must have been the same, but he was

old enough now, already thirty, to have accepted the boundaries of his life—his responsibilities as the father of a growing family, the limited success as an artist that he had achieved. He would have seen the painting suddenly, in a single moment: the woman Katje standing inside of it. She was standing there now, her eyes blue, her dress. She was bending over a letter, her hand resting against the curving arc of her stomach. It was a letter, he knew, from the young woman's brother, but in a painting, the painting he would do, the letter could come from anyone, even himself.

He would paint her as a young matron, receiving a love letter from a soldier, the light of Delft suffusing her face. He would put the model in the far corner of his studio, this time not even showing the window, but only the light of it. The girl would face in profile toward the light, and behind her would be the map of Holland, the only part of the "world" visible.

He would prepare his brushes and then get very quiet—as painting made him feel—as he always did before he began to work. Already he knew the center of it, the inward peace, the small wholeness at the core of it.

He would become light, the very motes in the air, and he would know her.

"Vermeer's Light" is a work of fiction that describes various works by the seventeenth-century Dutch master Johannes Vermeer. His paintings are collected by museums around the world, including the Rijksmuseum in Amsterdam, the Metropolitan Museum of Art in New York, the Frick Collection in New York, the National Gallery of Art in Washington D.C., and the Queen's Gallery in London.

Acknowledgments

I first of all must thank the literary journals and editors that chose to publish these stories, particularly *Southern Humanities Review* for giving so many of them a home—"The Beautiful Gaze," "The Calamity of Desire," (previously titled "The Death of Ria Munk), "Terminus," "Still Life with Cherries," and my novella "Women Bathing." Thank-you's also go to *Alaska Quarterly Review* for publishing "Vermeer's Light"; *The Shanghai Literary* Review for "Roman Glass" and *The Ekphrastic Review* for "The Birthday of the Infanta."

I also must acknowledge the extraordinary writer Kevin McIlvoy for his reading, insight, and belief in my work. His voice will remain inside of me forever. My early writing partner Dana Huebler was also instrumental in the start of many of these stories, and the exceptional writer Leslie Blanco, always generous with her reading and insight, first suggested that they belonged in a collection. Other writers who were invaluable for their support and insight include Deborah Bluestein, Linda Jassim, Kath Jesme, Sakae Manning, Chloe Martinez, Cynthia Prochaska, and Sonja Srinivasan.

It was the Los Angeles artist Douglas Wichert who told me that Annie Oakley had gone to Paris with Buffalo Bill—an idea I couldn't resist and so became the story "Terminus." An equal thank you to art-lover and longtime friend Sharon Hagan who alerted me to Gustav Klimt's paintings of Ria Munk.

The internet offered a wealth of knowledge to help me fictionalize the historical figures and events in this collection, but I also want to acknowledge: *Annie Oakley of the Wild West* by Walter Havighurst, *Buffalo Bill and Sitting Bull* by Bobby Bridger, *The First Moderns* by William Everdell, *Strapless* by Deborah Davis, and *Vermeer* by Arthur Wheelock, Jr.

The work of writer and filmmaker Judith Dancoff has always engaged itself with personal narrative as it confronts large social or political change. As a Pushcart nominated author, her short stories and essays have appeared in numerous journals including *The Georgia Review, Alaska Quarterly Review, Southern Humanities Review, The Shanghai Literary Review*, and elsewhere. Her prizes include residencies at Hedgebrook, the Virginia Center for Creative Arts, and the Djerassi Resident Artists Program, where she was the McElwee Family Fellow. Her earliest ambitions, however, were not in writing but in becoming a painter, a love that has found expression in this collection. She holds an MFA in fiction from the Warren Wilson Program for Writers and an MFA in filmmaking from UCLA. Her award-winning documentary "Judy Chicago & the California Girls" captures the birth of the feminist art movement in the early 1970s and is still of interest today. It has screened at and is owned by universities and museums around the world, including the Whitney Museum of American Art, the Metropolitan Museum of Art, the Museums of Contemporary Art in Los Angeles and Geneva, and the Victoria and Albert Museum in London.

www.ingramcontent.com/pod-product-compliance
Lightning Source LLC
Chambersburg PA
CBHW031434150426
43191CB00006B/515